THE CHAMPION WOMAN

7 SECRETS TO BECOMING A CHAMPION WOMAN

VERNON J. SHAZIER & SHAWN SHAZIER
FOREWORD BY: DR. HELEN TURNBULL

HOPE OF VISION PUBLISHING
BRIDGEPORT, CONNECTICUT

THE CHAMPION WOMAN
7 SECRETS TO BECOMING A CHAMPION WOMAN
Copyright © 2010 by Vernon J. Shazier

All rights reserved. No part of this book may be reproduced, copied, stored or transmitted in any form or by any means – graphic, electronic, or mechanical, including photocopying, recording, or information storage and retrieval systems without the prior written permission of Vernon J. Shazier or Hope of Vision Publishing except where permitted by law.

Hope of Vision Publishing a division of HOV, LLC.
www.Hopeofvisionpublishing.com
hopeofvision@gmail.com

Cover Design: Hope of Vision Designs

Editor: S.O.U.L.E Destiny, LLC

The Champion Leader, LLC
www.thechampionwoman.com
info@thechampionleader.com

For more information about special discounts for bulk purchases, please contact The Champion Leader or Hope of Vision Publishing.

ISBN 978-0-9753795-4-7
Library of Congress Number: 2010928859

Printed in the United States of America

Contents

Acknowledgements 5

Forward 6

Introduction 9

TCW Testimony: Brenda Atchinson 13

SECRET ONE   REDEFINING 17

TCW Testimony: Lisa Rogers Cherry 27

SECRET TWO   RESPECT 31

TCW Testimony: Beulah Glover 37

SECRET THREE   REQUIREMENT 41

TCW Testimony: Dr. Rosiland Osgood 48

SECRET FOUR   RELEASING 51

TCW Testimony: Marsha Freeman 60

SECRET FIVE   REACHING 63

TCW Testimony: Wanda Bolton-Davis 71

SECRET SIX   RESPONSIBILITY 73

TCW Testimony: Helen King 80

SECRET SEVEN   REWARD 83

TCW Testimony: Linda Scott 90

TCW Testimony: Pearl M. Davis ....…..…... 92

TCW Testimony: Gloria Ortiz ....…..… 96

TCW Testimony: Sharon Dunn ....…… 98

TCW Testimony: Teri Williams ....…..… 102

TCW Testimony: Renee Brown ....……104

TCW Testimony: Amanda Wright ..…..............…..…106

A Tale to Remember ....……108

Knowledge for You ....…......111

References ....….…118

About the Author ....……….. 121

Acknowledgements

The first and best part of my thanks always goes to God, the source of my intellect, creativity, and faith.

I must offer my heartfelt thanks to three wonderful people. First, I am grateful to you Shawn, my beautiful wife and the sunshine of my life. Your strength makes me stronger and the love you give to our family is infinite. I've been blessed with your everlasting patience and support as I continue to challenge and coach the world to live as champions. Secondly, Linda Poston in spite of your busy life as a mother, grandmother, and career-woman, you embraced this manuscript as a project of love. I appreciate all of your hard work and dedication. Finally, Starla Vaughns Cherin, my faithful friend and reader, I know your work is demanding yet you always found time to help with this project. I will forever be grateful to you.

For all the inspirational women who shared their Champion Woman testimonies, thank you.

Brenda Atchinson, Renee Brown, Lisa Rogers Cherry, Pearl Davis, Wanda Bolton-Davis, Sharon Dunn, Marsha Freedman, Beulah Glover, Helen King, Dr. Rosalind Osgood, Gloria Ortiz, Linda Scott, Terri Williams, Amanda Wright

FOREWORD

By: Dr. Helen Turnbull
www.humanfacets.com

While it is true there is a champion inside every woman, it is equally true many women struggle to find that champion. In fact, some women have such low self-esteem they have a hard time believing that there may be a champion lurking inside of them.

The surprising and little acknowledged fact among women is that even highly successful women can have low self-esteem and lead double lives, outwardly successful and inwardly worried that people will find out that they are frauds and more insecure than they portray.

The introduction of the Global Positioning System (GPS) receiver that is used when driving has been an enormous step forward in helping to navigate from one place to another. Getting lost is now a thing of the past. The use of the GPS receiver may likely decrease the chances of couples fighting about asking for direction. That is a hidden benefit of this tool. *"The Champion Woman"* can have a similar impact for the women who read it and follow the self-help guidelines.

There will be direct benefits and hidden benefits. You will find yourself inspired by the stories of other women, and in awe of the clarity with which the book lays out the stages of development towards becoming a Champion Woman. However, the hidden benefits will come from the cumulative impact on your life when you start behaving as a Champion Woman. People will wonder what happened to you. They will want to know if you won the lottery or if you have just met the love of your life. They will sense from your energetic field that something is different. As you start to read this book you cannot begin to imagine what the positive ripple effects will be. Like a pebble dropping in a pond, there will be a resounding impact – as the ripples from the pebble become a tsunami of championship proportions.

However, a word of caution: nothing worth having ever comes easily. If you are serious about this journey, you will need the courage to take a deeper look within. Be prepared. You may not like what you see, but have the courage to go there anyway. What is the story you tell yourself? Where are you deluding yourself? Is there alignment between your outer self and your inner self? Are you a drama queen? How do your actions affect others? What price do people pay to be in a relationship with you, and do you believe it's worth the cost?

Wherever you are on this journey, *"The Champion Woman"* offers a roadmap to finding the champion in you. Do the work, enjoy the journey, and be prepared to become a Champion Woman.

Introduction

WHY I WROTE THIS BOOK

For a man to write a book like this it demonstrates gratitude embedded in my heart and my true thankfulness for women. During a keynote speech to hundreds of educators, I encouraged them to continue in their commitment helping youth become champions. Afterwards, during my ride home, I reflected on the people in my life that helped me become a champion.

I reached for the tape recorder and began to speak the names of those who helped and continue to help me be a champion on the road of my life. At home, I played back the names and wrote them down on a piece of paper. While scanning them, I realized the majority were women. In other words, I have become a champion man because of the women in my life.

The first name on that list was the first woman in my life, my mom, Lee Shazier. She taught my siblings and me mental toughness. When I say she taught mental toughness, it was by watching the way she lived her life. When there was something that had to be done, my mom did it.

She raised four children while working multiple jobs. She worked at the elementary school we attended so we couldn't escape her. She played word games with us and used other educational tools to make sure we were academically astute.

She'd come home, cook, and assign our respective chores. We did them without complaint because of the respect we had for her and the authoritative presence she carried. She attended all of our school and sporting events. When we didn't have a car, my mom walked and caught the bus to work and to take care of her business. She is a fighter. Regardless of the obstacle, she showed no fear. Throughout her daily routine, we did not hear her say, 'I'm tired'.

She maintained self-respect at all times. After our dad left, she didn't allow a man to come to our house. Now that I think about it, we didn't even notice it. I'm sure she had a friend, but we didn't see him. Her first priority was raising her children to be productive individuals and to give back to the world.

She taught us to believe, first in God and then in ourselves. She taught us to believe God was on our side. I believed in God because I knew that is where my mom attained courage. She convinced us God was always on our side.

I chose the word champion because it's demonstrative of maximizing the potential talents and gifts God has given you.

This book contains secrets my wife Shawn and I know will serve as an aid to women in their journey as champions. It contains the testimonies of women who have encountered challenges in life that would have knocked down the best of us but not them. Their stories inspired me as I'm sure they will you.

It is my belief that every woman is created to be a Champion Woman.

"God created you to be a Champion Woman, don't settle for anything less."
-Vernon J. Shazier

7 SECRET SUMMARIES

SECRET #1 – REDEFINING

Acquire the motivating factor which will challenge you to pursue your goal of becoming a Champion Woman. Learn the secret of positive energy, allowing you to change negative thoughts into positive thoughts and actions. Find out what inspires you to be ambitious in your quest to become a Champion Woman.

SECRET #2 – RESPECT

Discover the single most important investment that you can make in your life. Discern if you are in a "basement relationship" and how to get out of one. Distinguish the steps needed to "Respect Yourself".

SECRET #3 – REQUIREMENT

What kind of relationships do you have? Discover the secret of challenging men to deal with you at your highest level. Find out what questions you should ask during the "getting to know you" stage.

SECRET #4 – RELEASING

Erykah Badu had a song called "Bag Lady". What type of baggage do you carry from relationship to relationship? Learn the steps of letting go of the past. Find out how to overcome hindrances and walk boldly into your future as a champion woman.

SECRET #5 - REACHING

"Dream your dreams and turn them into your passion." Identify what immobilizes you from reaching your goals. Discover how to conquer unplanned obstacles on your journey to become a Champion Woman.

SECRET #6 – RESPONSIBILITY

This chapter will teach you how to embrace your responsibility to yourself and others in becoming a Champion Woman. Learn how the trait of fear can be healthy and positive. Become accountable for your actions.

SECRET #7 – REWARD

You too can become an E.D.N.A. Find out the rewards others accomplished on their journey of becoming Champion Woman. Learn how to maximize your potential and reach "star" quality.

A CHAMPION WOMAN TESTIMONY

Brenda Atchinson

MY CHALLENGE

When asked to relate a challenge, I could think of many challenges in my life and they were varied, but the thing that strikes me most is the struggle of personal will. I am the kind of person who wants to have what I want right then and there. I wanted to jump full blown into success. I envisioned walking into whatever I was born to do; that included everything from going to college and completing college, to finding a career path, to becoming a successful business woman. I just wanted all of that to happen overnight.

I had to learn that anything you want in life is going to require you to put something into it, and it is a process. My mom says if you really want something, you need to put yourself through some trouble. I always thought that was cliché, but the more I thought about it, situations in life will bring about trouble, but you have to be willing to face each challenge and walk through your process.

I think that someone had it right when they said, "a journey of 1,000 miles starts with one step." My challenge was to go back to the beginning and start with one step toward whatever it was I wanted to do. This was a hard lesson for me to learn.

If I really wanted to do something and I didn't have the money or resources, I would just go and do it and hope everything turned out right. I didn't put a lot of time into planning. You know, life is divided between people who plan and people who do. I do think there is common ground for planning and doing, but I always wanted to do and let the planning take care of itself.

MY LESSON LEARNED

The lesson I learned is nothing happens in life that is accidental, haphazard, or coincidental. I've found that every experience I've had fits into God's grand scheme of things. As you find these challenges, you need to figure out where they fit in your life. I think every person has a purpose in life, and what you do in life is all directed toward that purpose.

We can run past some experiences and miss some of what we need to learn because we're trying to get to the destination, rather than taking time to enjoy the journey. Sometimes that means we run right past some lessons we need to learn. I think that's why we end up repeating what we didn't take time to do. We have to do things over because we didn't take them as part of our journey. When challenges occur, we need to sit down and figure out why we're being challenged at this time in our lives. Ask the question: What do I need to learn from this to grow and move forward?

MY MESSAGE FOR OTHERS

If you believe in God, a higher power, or feel you have been called to do certain things in your life, I believe He equips you to do what it takes to develop that gift. Our job, as human beings, is to find out what our purpose is and to align ourselves with that purpose. Part of having a gift is truly being able to give it. I think when you develop your gift you're in a position to pass it on to other people. You are never given a gift to keep it to yourself. We are not reservoirs. We are rivers --- gifts really flow through us.

You can experience happiness through developing your gift and using it to give back to help our community and take part in the general good of society. It's the type of happiness that is possibly lasting because you are walking in your purpose. It's not the type of happiness that depends on something outside of yourself to happen in order to make you happy. I believe true joy comes from walking in your purpose, for it ignites your passion. You know when you are really excited about doing something; you can't wait for the opportunity to do it. That's an indication you are doing what you ought to be doing and you feel good about it.

Always remember that life is not a destination. It's a journey, and a process.

SECRET #1

REDEFINING

"The thing that is really hard, and really amazing, is giving up on being perfect and beginning the work of becoming yourself."
-*Anna Quindlen*

The woman who thinks, talks, and walks like a winner usually is a winner. She maintains composure in stressful situations. She radiates self-assurance and projects confidence in every area of her life. What secret does she hold? She holds the secret of knowing who she is. She is a Champion Woman.

She doesn't rely on others, circumstances or the media to define her. She labels herself gifted, confident, powerful, positive, and intelligent. Do you see yourself as a Champion Woman? You must be convinced and confident in yourself and your gifts in order for others to see the champion you are.

I've encountered women who don't consider themselves valuable or pretty regardless of their physical beauty and accomplishments. What overshadows their idea of themselves is low self-esteem or what others think. They let the opinion of others shape and dictate their opinions of themselves.

I was in a relationship years ago with a very nice young lady. She took care of her business and was beautiful and tall enough to be a model. In most of her relationships, however, she allowed herself to experience physical and psychological abuse. She didn't think much of herself. The guys she dated in her previous relationships messed her up so badly she could look in the mirror and not see herself as she was.

She thought she was insignificant, not having a lot to offer in life. It became work for me to "build her up" constantly. It was amazing to me and mind-boggling how a woman, nearly six-feet-tall, beautiful and seemingly confident could think she didn't matter. She became an immense burden to all around her. There are women who don't realize their intrinsic value. They allow others to steal their value.

> "Our greatest weakness lies in giving up. The most certain way to succeed is always to try just one more time." - *Thomas Edison*

The first requirement in redefining yourself is self-perception. How do you see yourself, not physical beauty, but inner beauty? Take a few minutes for inner introspection. Thoughtfully ask yourself these questions:

1. What is your definition of a Champion Woman?
2. What are your motivations?
3. List three adjectives to describe yourself:
    a.
    b.
    c.

4. List three things you are good at doing:
    a.
    b.
    c.
5. List three ways others would describe you:
    a.
    b.
    c.
6. What are your top three goals?
    a.
    b.
    c.
7. What is your definition of success?
    a.
    b.
    c.

Great, how did it go? Assessing yourself can be difficult at times. We don't always see ourselves clearly. Our paradigms, the way we see things, can be limited because they are perceptions based on past experiences. Your prototype or paradigms can be altered or changed by expanding your horizons.

To see things from a different perspective, you have to acquire and interpret information from diverse views. If you continue to scrutinize life from limited opinions, your ideas and your motivations will also be limited. Broadening your paradigms increases your knowledge and creativity to successfully complete your goal to become a champion.

There is a woman, Edna, who seemed stuck in a life fraught with danger and misguided possibilities. Engulfed in a life of lies and thievery, Edna stole a few of her family members' credit cards and checks and forged their signatures. Even while attending funerals she would help herself to the pocketbooks left on the pews, while the owners were celebrating, offering congratulations, or paying their respects. In her teens and early 20s Edna went to jail for forgery.

Today, at the age of 60-plus, Edna fully supports herself with honest employment and is an integral part of a management team. She could have easily continued as a criminal, but she chose to change her paradigm. Yet those around her still see her as a thief.

Every time a family member mentions Edna's name, they speak of her as being selfish, devious, and unreliable. Her family quite often tells the story of Edna's pickpocket days. They tell it at family gatherings, reunions, weddings, and funerals. They will not let it die.

People who didn't know Edna's past describe her as intelligent, charismatic, trustworthy, solid, caring, and friendly. She always has a word of encouragement or wisdom. One co-worker recalls a time when Edna stepped in to help her. Payroll hadn't entered the young lady's hours and she didn't receive a paycheck. Like many people in these economic times, the young lady anticipated being paid and had already written checks against her account.

Payroll determined it would take up to five business days for her check to be processed. Frantic, the young woman went to Edna for help because Edna worked in administration, and she hoped Edna could contact payroll and expedite the process. Unfortunately, she couldn't. Edna opened her own pocketbook, retrieved her personal checkbook, and wrote the young lady a check that would cover her outstanding checks. Edna told her when she received her paycheck from payroll she could pay her back.

I'm not suggesting you lend or give money away. What I am saying is Edna had enlarged her perimeters by changing her paradigms. She not only became a trustworthy individual, but she trusted others. Edna was in the process of redefining herself. Instead of a borrower or thief, Edna became a lender and a benefactor.

Today Edna describes what she did to redefine herself. "I am an overcomer, an eternal student, and eternally grateful. I didn't always see myself like that. Edna reminisced. "In my youth, I would have described myself as troubled, unworthy, and unlovable. You see, I was the quintessential middle child. My father passed when I was 12 years old. He had been my greatest supporter. My mother struggled with life after his passing; her will to live died right along with him. I felt as if I were invisible and made several regrettable mistakes in my life. I couldn't allow them to keep me in the past. I had to find a way to forgive myself and to forget myself, the old self. I paid my debt to society and was given a chance to move beyond what had taken place years prior. One day at a time, I redefined myself. I stopped looking back and started to look forward to new and achievable possibilities."

We all have skeletons in our past. There are unfavorable times in life that family members, friends, or your own personal reflections make it hard to bury them. Stop allowing your past performances to mandate the end of your story. Edna changed the results of her story. Her self-analysis is self-measured. Use the questions above to make an evaluation of who you are and who you would like to become.

Measure your strengths and weaknesses. Be honest with yourself. Who can possibly know you better than you do? Who is with you 24 hours a day, 7 days a week, and 365 days a year? You control your own definition. No one else can make the changes in your life that you are striving to attain. No one can do it for you.

One of the questions you were asked in the self-analysis was, how do you define success? Does excessive material gain exemplify success? Does a college degree or a high-paying job illustrate victory to you?

Ralph Waldo Emerson, a 19th-century philosopher and leader in the Transcendentalist movement, describes success in part as the ability to laugh often and much, to win the respect of intelligent people and the affection of children. It earns the appreciation of honest critics and endures the betrayal of false friends.

Success appreciates beauty and finds the best in others. Success leaves the world a bit better, whether by birthing a healthy child, tending a garden patch, or working to redeem a social condition.

Success is the knowing that even one life has breathed easier because you have lived; that beloved is success. Edna changed her definition of success from illegally obtaining material wealth to helping others and, in the process, gained respect for herself and the admiration of others.

Mr. Emerson had several key words in his account of success. Remember these words as you reflect on your own personal definition: RESPECT, LAUGHTER, APPRECIATION, ENDURANCE, and AFFECTION.

Becoming a Champion Woman doesn't magically happen. It is a thoughtful process that requires setting personal goals. There are no mysterious formulas. Championship status unfolds as we commit ourselves to consistently doing something every day that builds upon our idea of a Champion Woman.

There is a game many of us played as children called Connect the Dots. On a page in a book lies a multitude of dots with numbers or alphabets next to them. The object of the game is to connect the dots in numerical or alphabetical order to create a picture. The same is applicable with our goals to become a Champion Woman.

Connect the dots of your daily goals to allow the picture of the Champion Woman to be revealed. It is a daily process that is a commitment to yourself. Painstakingly connecting the dots of your life until the final picture materializes requires love, endurance, and persistence.

You know what the final picture is, because you just defined it with the initial question. To bring championship to fruition, there are small, sometimes seemingly insignificant steps we have to take. There is no way to eliminate the process and grab the prize without the work.

The beginning of the journey toward becoming a Champion Woman is redefining yourself on a cognitive level. Your task requires you to reach into your subconscious and grasp what motivates you. Once you've captured those aspects of inspiration, there is a subsequent question you should consider: What inspires you to be ambitious in your goal of becoming a Champion Woman?

Edna's motivating revelation emerged during a stint in jail. She realized the 6x8 cell was larger than the walls surrounding her mind. Edna was held captive by her own "stinking" thinking. How could she become a champion when she didn't think she was worthy? She viewed herself as a failure, not a champion.

Daily we have to connect our thoughts to positive reinforcement. Edna's thoughts, like many of ours, were mostly negative, making her outlook on life pessimistic. That doesn't mean we are destined to be miserable. The process is to build daily on a habit of thinking positive and using possibility thinking.

Here are some ways to change your "stinking" thinking into productive, positive, possibility thinking:

Reject faulty philosophies. Periodically stop and evaluate your viewpoints. If you find your thoughts are mainly negative, try to find a way to put a positive spin on them. Think of the possibilities and know you are worthy.

Value peoples differences. The essence of valuing differences is being able to recognize we all see the world not as it is, but as we are. Our world is based on our personal paradigms and our perceptions. When we recognize that people have different perceptions and we are open to listening to them, our paradigms shift.

Follow a healthy lifestyle. Exercise at least three times a week to positively affect mood and reduce stress. Follow a healthy diet to fuel your mind and body. Learn to manage stress.

Surround yourself with positive people. Make sure those in your life are positive, supportive people you can depend on to give helpful advice and feedback. Negative people, those who believe they have no power over their lives, or those who think they have power over your life, might increase your stress level and make you doubt your ability to manage stress in healthy ways.

Change negative thoughts to positive thoughts. When negative thoughts bombard your mind, immediately change the thought. Even when circumstances seem dim, do not let your mind dwell on the negative. Be your own best cheerleader and say to yourself, "I am a champion woman. I am a winner. I am successful. I am worthy. I generate positive energy."

Fill out the following chart (I've given you an example to start you out):

NEGATIVE THOUGHTS	CHAMPIONSHIP THOUGHTS
I've never done it before.	It's an opportunity to learn something new.

Let me emphasize this is a process; don't expect to become a Champion Woman overnight. Practice, practice, practice, and connect each dot. Soon you'll be looking through rose-colored glasses, seeing the world around you in a positive mode.

"The longer I live, the more I realize the impact of attitude on life. Attitude, to me, is more important than the past, than education, than money, than what people say or do. The remarkable thing is that we have a choice every day regarding the attitude we will embrace. We cannot change our past ... we cannot change the fact that people will act in a certain way. We cannot change the inevitable. The only thing we can do is play on the one string we have and that is our attitude. I am convinced that life is 10 percent what happens to us and 90-percent how we react to it."

- Charles Swindoll

Let a positive attitude be a motivating factor you acquire as you go through the daily process of redefining yourself as a Champion Woman.

TCW
DEFINING MOMENTS

What is the most important concept you learned in this chapter?

Why is this concept important to you?

What are three steps you will take to implement this concept into your life?

A CHAMPION WOMAN TESTIMONY

Lisa Rogers Cherry

MY CHALLENGE

One of my challenges was growing up without my father in my home. I did not feel as if it was an issue when I was young. I didn't realize how it affected me until I got to law school. There, all the minority students had mentors who were professors, but mine was the school psychologist.

Throughout my life growing up, there was always a strong, black female head in the household. My grandmother was the mother of 15 children and my grandfather was killed when my mom was born, so she didn't have that father figure in the home either.

My grandmother always taught us all to be strong and never go to anyone outside of the home or our race with our problems. You took your problems to God, go have prayer, talk to the pastor, or something like that. You never went to talk to strangers.

Friends would talk to their mentors when they faced challenges, but mine being the school psychologist drove me to run the other way when I saw her. I thought, "No way am I going to tell this white woman anything about me." Plus, I had been taught that it was taboo to talk about personal experiences with strangers.

One day, while near her office, she asked me to come in and that 20 minutes virtually changed my life. We exchanged introductions and I got to know her better. Soon I felt comfortable. We clicked with each other and later became friends.

I talked about my family and being from a single-parent home. I talked about my feelings toward my father; although I never really considered my thoughts about him. It was just a void because he was never there. He was dead in my mind.

It wasn't until I started visiting her and talking about fathers and the guys I dated in school that I realized I had issues I wasn't dealing with. There were abandonment issues and fears of certain things because I didn't have that male role model in my home.

Growing up I was ashamed to talk about it. People would ask, "Why doesn't your dad ever come to things?" I blamed myself. He called every three years or so and sent a birthday card once in a while. On father-and-daughter day at Spellman College he said he would come and didn't show up. Always false promises: "I'm going to do" this or that and never doing any of it.

I started to see my mentor regularly and began to write about my feelings. Some of it dealt with men or how I didn't deal with men; what I looked for and how I treated guys, and sometimes even how I allowed them to treat me. All of it was a result of the lack of relationship I had with my father.

MY LESSON LEARNED

That summer I started doing research on the topic. I found it fascinating that I had been dealing with this – or not dealing with this – for 20 years, and it was negatively impacting me.

I approached a professor who taught about women and their relationships to help me formulate a survey. I interviewed 125 women and found they all had issues with their father pertaining to a lack of a relationship with their father. I was amazed to see how different people dealt with things although they had similar experiences.

Next, the mentor gave me the exercise to write a letter about everything I was feeling – all of the anger, hurt, and mistrust – and then put it up somewhere. Instead, I mailed it to my father, letting him know exactly how I felt.

Later still, before I delivered my daughter, my husband suggested I mend fences with my father. I said, "What do I want to do that for? I'm a grown woman now." I didn't see the need. He insisted I do it because he didn't want me or our daughter to have issues of dealing with this negative void in my life.

I called my father and we agreed to talk. I taped the hour and a half long conversation. I talked about how I felt and he talked about how he felt. It was a great conversation. I never imagined some of the things he shared with me. It never even crossed my mind why he did certain things or was not a part of my life.

He said he didn't know how to love and how to treat women. The final question he had for me was, would I be able to forgive him? At the time I couldn't say yes because I wanted to mean what I said. It was going to take some time.

I prayed and asked God to help the hurt and help me learn how to love this man. Forgive him for what he's done, not done, or not done for me or with me the whole gamut of our relationship – or lack of one.

I was finally able to say, "Yes, I forgive you." I could really feel it in my heart and I could honestly say, "I loved him." We developed a relationship and became friends. He was encouraging, he quoted scriptures that were appropriate and had the right thing to say when I needed it.

After the third year of our time together, he was killed in a car accident and I was asked to deliver the eulogy at his funeral. I was able to do it with a clear conscious and good heart because of the time we spent together.

MY MESSAGE TO OTHERS

Don't keep things to yourself and walk around with bottled-up anger. Find someone you can trust and talk to. You have to talk to someone who won't judge you so you are able to say exactly how you feel and know it won't get all over town.

The process helped me open up. Now I don't feel like I'm in the world all by myself, or like I did something wrong. Before they saw Lisa, but they never saw the hurting Lisa. No one would ever see that. It helped me in my marriage and with my daughter to teach her to talk about things and better express herself. Before when people said they are going to do something, I just said, "Yeah, right." If my husband promised something, even something small, if it didn't go just as he said I would, "really get on him." I especially got crazy about promises to our daughter.

I had to learn to let that go and for awhile it was difficult. I had to realize he, my husband, was not my dad.

SECRET #2

RESPECT

"When you respect yourself, you become the kind of woman who others respect."
-*Vernon J. Shazier*

Growing up as a young man, I didn't really respect women. It's not that I set out to be disrespectful or uncaring. I wasn't taught to value and admire the opposite sex. My purpose for forging relationships with women was limited to the physical – a purpose I thought was fulfilling to both of us. I had no expectations beyond the bedroom and if they wanted more than that, I wasn't the right person. I didn't hide my way of thinking. Get on board or don't. Be with me or without me. Just don't try to change me, because I am who I am.

As a result of my way of thinking, I was in different relationships with women who didn't respect themselves, thus allowing me to treat them, as some would say, cold and uncaring. What I thought was great interaction didn't quite achieve relationship status. My connection with others never seemed to get off the ground floor or go above the belt. I had what I coin "basement relationships" with them. I wasn't abusive or violent. I would just come and go as I wanted. I always had a "trust" issue. I never let women, or anyone else for that matter, get close to me. This issue continued until the third year after I had become a Christian. It is easy for men to have relationships with women who don't think much of themselves. There are no expectations. They settle for anything.

In the meantime, maybe I can help you with the respect issue. I would like to encourage you to make the single most important investment you will ever make in your life. This investment is more important than your finances, your spouse, your children, your job, or your automobile. It's more potent than any tangible item you might have or adore. This phenomenal venture will equip you to reach the goal of becoming a Champion Woman. If you don't invest in this, you might never achieve any objective you pursue in life. I'll even go as far as to say, that without this, you might never truly be happy.

Now that I have your attention, let me tell you a story I heard just the other day. It's about Beatrice the Bagger.

Beatrice works in a local grocery store bagging groceries. With the recession, profits were down and management was concerned they may have to cut positions. As a last resort, management had an outside consultant come in.

Of all things, the consultant decided to train the employees in the art of good customer service. Many of the employees grumbled, wondering how good customer service could help them keep their jobs, or in your case, help you succeed in becoming a Champion Woman. Well, Beatrice the Bagger, being young and quite inexperienced listened attentively to the consultant's speech.

At the conclusion of the hour-long seminar, the instructor gave each employee a homework assignment.

HOMEWORK
Think of a way you can personally make each customer's visit so enjoyable, they will continue to shop at this store.

When Beatrice got home that evening, she was stumped. She couldn't imagine how she, a lowly bag person, could make a difference. After talking with her mother regarding her assignment, Beatrice came up with an idea. She worked late into the night, completing her task. The next day, Beatrice arrived early to work. Many of the other employees were there with smiles plastered on their faces, going an extra mile to help the customers complete their shopping spree. As always, Beatrice was courteous and pleasant.

However, as Beatrice bagged customer's groceries, she slipped a piece of paper into their bags. When the customers got home from a tiring day of shopping, at the bottom of their bag was a note of encouragement and thanks from Beatrice. As the weeks progressed, the grocery store manager noticed that one line was loaded with customers. Over the intercom, she called for additional clerks to open. Even with additional help, one line kept increasing. The manager personally went over to let customers know that other lines would service them, but they stayed put.

Finally, the manager asked why they wanted to stay in a long line, when other lines were almost empty. "For Beatrice's beautiful words of encouragement," they said one after the other. "Sometimes I don't even need groceries, but will come in and pick something up just to receive her notes." So, you ask again, what does Beatrice's customer service commitment have to do with the single most powerful investment that you can ever make in your life?

Customer service should start at home first. We ourselves are our first and foremost customer. The single most important investment that you can make in your life is to invest in yourself, mentally, physically, spiritually, and socially.

Your body, mind, and spirit are the only instruments you have to deal with and contribute to life. You are the instrument of your own performance. To be effective, to succeed in life, to become a Champion Woman, you need to recognize the importance of taking time regularly to express and exercise all four motivations of your nature.

In other words, a major step in becoming a Champion Woman is to respect yourself.

Respect yourself physically
- Exercise
- Nutrition
- Stress management

The physical dimension involves caring effectively for our physical body, eating the right foods, getting sufficient rest and relaxation and exercising on a regular basis.

Respect yourself spiritually
- Values
- Ethics
- Commitments

The spiritual investment is your value system. We all have a belief system we are committed to that dictates where our values come from.

Respect yourself mentally
- Reading
- Visualizing
- Writing

Author Stephen J. Covey says, "The person who doesn't read is no better off than the person who can't read." You have to visualize being a Champion Woman in order to become one. Whatever your specific goal, picture the scenario and see yourself acting successfully in it. Writing is a powerful way to keep our mental faculties sharp. One way of doing this is to keep a journal of your thoughts and experiences to promote mental clarity, exactness, and context.

Before life's journey wears you out, do as Beatrice did. Invest your time and energy into giving the best customer service you have to offer. Start with yourself. This isn't a new revelation, but a pertinent discovery. It is a proactive approach in achieving championship status. You must take time out for yourself: renewing yourself mentally, physically, spiritually, and socially. Before you know it the words setback, hesitate, hindrance or holdup won't define you. You'll soon be known as that Champion Woman who can always be counted on to come through on time. Take the step of being proactive by participating daily in the production of your life. After all, you are the main character.

TCW
DEFINING MOMENTS

What is the most important concept you learned in this chapter?

Why is this concept important to you?

What are three steps you will take to implement this concept into your life?

A CHAMPION WOMAN TESTIMONY

Beulah Glover

MY CHALLENGE

The decision to return to college after becoming the mother of three toddlers, ages 3, 2, and a few months old, was a challenge for me. My obstacles were my finances, my husband was in graduate school, wife of the senior pastor, and my children were all under the age of 4.

Attaining my education was one of the things I was very desirous to do in my life. I also promised my dad I would complete my education. I attended one year of college after high school, then my husband and I were married, and 10 years later I still had not returned to complete my degree.

After my husband accepted his call into the ministry, we moved to Daytona Beach, where we didn't know anyone. After completing Bethune Cookman University, he continued on to the theological seminary in Atlanta. He drove to Atlanta from Daytona every week; traveling six hours there and back while leaving me at home with three babies.

Although the timing and the finances were not favorable, I continued trusting and believing in God, knowing that through Him I could do all things. After much prayer and confirmation, I learned this was the right time. I said, "God, if this is what you want then you will open the door for me."

I finished my college entrance papers, the financial data, and loan papers which should have been submitted in March of the previous year in August and I wanted to enter in September. I hand delivered my paperwork to the Registrar's Office, and they said, "Oh, Mrs. Glover, it's too late. We have already accepted most of the papers for those entering in the fall." I replied, "Oh well, if it doesn't go through I'll be ready for January."

I left it in the Lord's hands. The registrar called me before we returned home. The Lord moved within five days to have all my paperwork accepted. All doors where open for me, from my finances to the classes I needed.
The lady at the financial aid office said, "This has never happened before. We haven't ever seen anything like this, everything opening up at the last minute."

I started college with three little babies, no money, and my husband away. I graduated four years later *magna cum laude*. God helped me come through it with flying colors.

MY LESSON LEARNED

I learned the faithfulness of God, the reliability of God, and the proof that He is truly a God of His word. He will open doors for you that no man can close. He is on time and He is never late. He will direct your path in a way that is best for you if you are praying in His will. I prayed to let God's will be done, not Beulah's will.

As I reflect, I understand it was necessary for me to experience the faithfulness of God opening doors. I have been able to witness too many young women, mothers, and pastors wives. They say, "Oh, I can't do it. I have these kids and no funds." I can say with assurance having already walked that route, God will open doors for you. There is nothing too hard for God. Yes, you can do it if you are determined and a prayer warrior. Does it get tough? Yes, it does get hard but God's grace is sufficient to carry you through the challenges.

I learned with prayer and perseverance I could prevail over many obstacles. One obstacle I overcame was having a vehicle with heat, but lacked the luxury of air conditioning. However, I'm thankful for the traveling mercy while on the road with my small children. You learn the luxury isn't in the vents, it's in the covering of God's mighty hand. I'd trade comfort for safety provided by God any day. He kept the children without colds and me well with only three or four hours of sleep a night taking care of the household. He moved in a mighty way in all facets of our lives.

Parishioners would ask, "Why are you going back to school now, pastor has it." However, my mother said, "It's better to have it and not need it, then to need it and not have it." It was something I wanted to do for myself.

Little did I know my education would help me in the work I'm doing now as administrator of Mount Bethel Christian Academy, as well as ministering to hurting women. Many of these women think they can't accomplish their goals because of certain obstacles, but I tell them if I did it you can do it.

MY MESSAGE TO OTHERS

There is absolutely nothing too hard for our God to help us overcome. God helps us through our faith and perseverance. You can't give up. You will accomplish all you desire if you set your mind, heart, and spirit to it. You must believe that God is God, all powerful, and you must believe He will accomplish what He sets out to do with your life. He will complete it. He will bring it through for you.

My living scripture is Romans 8:28, "We know that all things work together for good to them that love God, to them who are the called according to his purpose."

Remember: It is not your purpose, but God's purpose.

SECRET #3

REQUIREMENT

"A woman will never find genuine happiness with a man who is only interested in sex."
-*Shawn Shazier*

Secret 3: The Requirement is not about being an elitist; however, you cannot go through life allowing men to deal with you primarily through a physical relationship. Many women are in relationships based on the physical and are not having intellectual conversations with men. When you first laid eyes on the man of your so-called dreams, you saw a big, strapping, muscular specimen with curly hair and teeth so white they sparkled as he smiled just for you. Your first thought wasn't "I wonder if he is ambitious and has goals in his life?" No, your first thought may have been in line with the study of basement principles. Basement means dealing with you at your lowest level -- sex.

I hope you understand that being with a man has to be more than whether he makes you feel good and satisfies you physically. Does he mentally or physically abuse you? Sometimes women allow physical pleasure to blind them to reality.

For example, a woman who is financially independent often doesn't require a man to rise above a basement relationship. The man you are in a relationship with may not wish to go anywhere. It can be very challenging for independent women who don't need a mate for financial reasons to demand men to deal with them at their highest level.

Your highest level is above your waist and in your brain. Your partner may be able to gratify you sexually but that shouldn't be the primary qualification. You find that he's good in bed, but as your relationship progresses you discover the connection is incomplete. What kind of relationship do you have with this person other than in the bedroom?

Psychologically you need a man who is willing to communicate with you. One who has goals and aspirations and cares about something besides self.

To establish a positive, balanced relationship women must require men to communicate with them both mentally and spiritually. It's in a man's nature to function below the waist, to deal with you at your lowest level. Sometimes a woman must demand that he meets her at the highest level, otherwise he will continue to do what he has always done. For your relationship to elevate from the basement level you have to have a meaningful, valued affiliation; it can't be predicated on sex alone.

Requiring a man to deal with you at your highest level begins with you. You have to know what you want, because the man knows what he wants when he comes to you. You have to demonstrate that you are intelligent and he has to deal with you spiritually and mentally. Talk with him about your ambitions and goals, the dreams you have and ask him to share his. These types of conversations will help guard you from being blinded by a man's physical attribute.

You have to require that a man give you the type of relationship you want.

No one wants to talk about this, but today it is imperative that each partner be tested for HIV and STDs.

Before you get involved, make the one you are attracted to get tested.

Another significant question to ask in the "getting to know you" stage is to find out what his credit score is. There's a commercial that shows a young man singing and playing the guitar in the basement of a house. He sings that he and his new bride couldn't get the house they wanted because her credit score was low. He wished he had asked her before they were married. He would have been living in a nice condominium instead of living in her parent's basement. I'm not saying that you shouldn't pursue a relationship because of an unfavorable credit score, but the more knowledge you have about your potential partner the better equipped you will be to decide if he's the one.

Score yourself on relationship building. Pay attention to what you want in a relationship and stick to it. I understand compromise, but there are certain things you know you can or cannot tolerate. Ignoring those signs can be detrimental in the end. If you will not put up with someone who smokes cigarettes, don't think you can change him. Trust me; your sweet loving will not overpower his urge to smoke. There are little nuances about each of us that are a part of our personality. Recognize your limitations.

If you don't challenge him to deal with you on a higher level, you will get stuck in a basement relationship and all the negative qualities will come out after you've been drawn in emotionally. That's when so many women cry out, "I wish I had that conversation with him earlier, before we got physical. Now it's more challenging to talk about it. I found out recently that he hasn't had a job in nine months. He doesn't have any dreams. He has no ambition whatsoever. He's not interested in going to church, to a movie, to dinner, or to anything."

You wish that you had known how he sees himself as a man, the spiritual component. It can be difficult to move beyond the physical and sexual relationship once you're involved. I understand that he knows how to touch you, but in reality that's only for five minutes.

A part of the requirement is to understand that you have more to offer and you bring more to the table than just your body. A man can get that from several places. You have to stand up and look him in his eye, face to face and demand that he deal with you at your highest level. There's more to you than what's below your waist. This is real. It's important. We allow men to stay on their knees (that's a metaphor of dealing from the waist down). Let him know there is much more for him to discover and get to know – and it's above your waist. There is no mouth below the waist to talk or converse with. There is a reason why the brain is above the waist. The reason so many men don't want to deal with you above the waist is because that's where the brain is. They don't want to be challenged on an intellectual level. They only want physical satisfaction.

It is your responsibility, Champion Woman, to delay gratification.

Men have to understand that God made you a whole woman. If God only wanted you to be dealt with below your waist, He didn't have to make you the way He did: whole mind, body, and spirit. God created you to be a whole woman, so why would you allow men to deal with you as if you are half a woman? Deal with me in my full totality, my highest level. Take me out somewhere. Escort me to rooms other than the bedroom. If you don't demand that he deals with you as a whole woman, the only room he'll escort you to is the bedroom. Let him know there are other rooms you wish to explore. Some women in relationships can't get the man to go to the movies. They feel they did enough of that when they were courting. Now he's dealing with you at your lowest level.

What do you do after the five minutes are up? How does he engage you after that? He can only engage you at your lowest level for five minutes. What do you do with the other minutes, hours, or days? Do you just look at each other? If so, you are disconnected. There's an intellectual component to you as well. You want to do things socially outside of the house. When you are in a basement relationship, a man is only dealing with you at your lowest level – and that's it.

Many men have been coached and trained to have basement relationships. A woman walks by a man and the man says, "She's fine – look at her," as he looks at her physical attributes. How many men say, "Look at her spirit, her conversation, her intellect," when considering a potential mate? They've been culturally conditioned to focus below the waist.

The first place the man puts his hand is on the hips, on the butt, but not on her head. Why? Because the average man has been trained and coached to have basement relationships.

One evening during the first three years of our marriage, my wife asked me the "Why don't you?" questions. "Why don't you call me during the day? Why don't you ask me how did my day go? Why don't you give me a hug or kiss when you get home from work?" My response usually indicated that wasn't my style, so don't try to make me into another man since I'm not that kind of man.

Then one night my wife started crying and moaned for five hours nonstop. I had to go into the other room. She continuously lamented "I want you to treat me like I'm your queen," but that was not my nature. I didn't know how to do it. I wasn't trained or coached on how to have a relationship above the waist. I was in the basement and didn't know how to get out nor was I even sure I wanted to get out and elevate myself.

That night her feelings and words touched me and did something drastic to me inside. To save my marriage and make the woman I loved happy, I had to redefine myself. Each night for the next three months or so, on my way home from work I had a talk with myself.

I reprogrammed myself by asking myself the "Why don't you?" questions. I practiced asking her how was her day. I saw myself giving her a hug or kiss when I arrived home. I anticipated her excitement as I asked her out on a date.

Why the sudden change? Why did I feel the need to change my label? She demanded that I deal with her on her highest level, intellectually and spiritually. I knew I would lose her if I didn't meet her requirements. I knew she was precious, valuable and should be handled in a delicate, nourishing, and loving way.

At this stage in this book, a Champion Woman is emerging. You are that woman who thinks, walks and talks like a winner. You are learning to maintain your composure even in stressful situations. You are doing something every day to make yourself better. You Champion Women are self-confident and poised.

You know the secret of redefining who you are – the secret of the power of respect. As you move forward in life, you require men to deal with you at your highest level. You possess the secret of requiring others to elevate to your position instead of you bowing to theirs. You have redefined yourself, understanding that you are valued and deserving of respect.

TCW
DEFINING MOMENTS

What is the most important concept you learned in this chapter?

Why is this concept important to you?

What are three steps you will take to implement this concept into your life?

A CHAMPION WOMAN TESTIMONY

Dr. Rosiland Osgood

MY CHALLENGE

I was born to teenage parents, raised in the church, went to college and came out a drug and alcohol addict. A two-time convicted felon, I knew what it's like to fight ants and rodents for a meal from the trash dumpster. Once clean, God helped me become an avenger for Christ. When diagnosed with lymphoma, a cancer of the throat, my husband of 18 years divorced me because he did not want to care for a sick wife. Just a few months before my divorce, my grandmother, my rock and the woman who raised me, passed away.

Grace and God's unmerited favor saved me as I redefined myself to embrace a life filled with purpose and a mission to help others. I emerged from a drug addicted two-time convicted felon to a scholar with five academic degrees. This I've earned despite being told by my third grade teacher that I would never read or write. Today, I work as an adjunct professor at Nova Southeastern University, the CEO of a nonprofit organization, and a practicing minister of the Good News.

MY LESSON LEARNED

Parenting is key and my grandmother never gave up on me. She continued to see the good in me regardless of how I looked on the outside. My grandmother saw who I was in Christ. She saw me in the future. Not the 65-pound soaking wet drug addict. She recognized Rosalind, the CEO of Dr. Osgood Ministry International.

A lesson I learned from my struggles is God loves us so much that He will always come in the cave and get us out.

MY MESSAGE TO OTHERS

Understand that God is willing and wanting to release blessings to us. There is nothing we can do that is too bad for God to give up on us. In the Bible, Genesis 3 tells the story of Adam and Eve. They disobeyed God yet as they were walking in the garden in the cool of the day, He sought after them.

Every day wake up to overcome obstacles by optimizing opportunities; you will obtain outstanding outcomes. Everything with God is outstanding, great, and grand. The power of the Holy Ghost allows us to overcome the obstacles of life. God sustains and moves us. Your life's party is just beginning.

SECRET #4

RELEASING

"When you find peace within yourself, you become the kind of person who can live at peace with others."
-*Peace Pilgrim*

Secret 4 is releasing to live. It's about releasing yourself from past hurts and destructive or unproductive relationships. An unproductive relationship is one where you have exhausted all attempts to cultivate the relationship, and it is clear that your mate is not able or unwilling to cooperate and make the necessary contributions and sacrifices for your relationship to reach championship status.

Past hurts carried around in your mind hinder your progress and your relationships mentally, physically and spiritually. They become obstacles to making future strides and reaching your highest potential. They are mind blocks that hide the good in your life.

Monique Rider's story is of releasing to live and the courage to love herself more than she loved someone else. She is an example of a woman who attempted to cultivate a relationship despite her and her children's suffering.

"Beating the Odds" By Monique Rider

I met Joe when I was 15. We were married eight months after we met. I was 16 and he was 19. I could not drive and I dropped out of school right after the wedding.

This was the beginning of eight years of struggling, sacrificing, and heartache.

I became more and more dependent on my husband. He became the center of my life. I had very few friends and no outside interests. I am still confused as to whether he made me become dependent on him, or if I allowed it to happen. Maybe it was a little of both. I was young and vulnerable and needed to depend on someone. To keep me dependent on him he used mind games, intimidation, manipulation, and guilt trips. He wouldn't allow me to have a checking account or credit cards. He had me believing I could not handle the money – that I wouldn't be able to balance the checkbook and I would run up the charge cards. He told me we were always behind on our bills because I couldn't figure the budget correctly. He controlled the money and the bills never got paid.

He rarely let me go anywhere alone. He said there were too many weirdoes out there who could hurt me. Eventually, either I went places with him or I stayed home. I was afraid to walk across the street to the park – so I never went. He did not make me submit by becoming violent with me. However, he was violent with other people. He was from an abusive family. His violence often emerged when he was drinking or on drugs.

I witnessed many of his fights and beatings. I saw him break the glass out of vehicles with a baseball bat. Even though he was not violent with me, maybe just seeing the violence was what made me submit. Various weapons were kept throughout the house. Clubs, baseball bats, and guns were hidden behind the furniture. He slept with a sharpened machete next to his side of the bed. These weapons were used in his acts of violence against other people.

He had quite a long police record and it seemed like we were forever paying his fines and restitution. If he could hold a job for more than six months, he was doing well. We moved around a lot because either we couldn't pay the rent, were kicked out, or Joe couldn't get along with the landlords. He constantly thought other people were out to get him. He thought the whole world was against him. Each negative thing that happened to him, he blamed on someone else. He completely isolated me from people. We moved away from my family and didn't get along with his. He couldn't get along with our friends for very long periods of time. During an argument that was his fault – where he did something wrong – it was usually me that ended up apologizing.

    I felt as if I was the one who did something wrong. He would accuse me of doing things of which he was guilty: jealousy, over possessiveness, poor managing skills with money, insecurity. I felt as if I had to strive to prove him wrong and gain his respect. It was emotionally draining. I felt like I was making one sacrifice after another. I forgave him each time for being arrested, never coming home, or squandering the rent money.

    For eight years, we struggled and never had a thing to show for it. Meanwhile, I became more and more dependent on him. I didn't drive. If I worked, it caused problems so I would quit. Any type of stress would cause his drinking to increase. He would drink and take drugs in binges. His behavior was very unpredictable. I felt as if things had to be just perfect for him, so he wouldn't get upset.

    Our first daughter was born in 1984. The stress of the new baby caused another drinking binge which eventually led to Joe being arrested. He was in a fight and charged with assault and destruction of property. Joe was between jobs most of the time. He refused to get unemployment or help from Social Services. We lived off borrowed money or side jobs he picked up here and there.

Our second daughter was born in 1986. I finally decided to go back to work. Thinking it would help our financial situation, I found a job that paid very well and had excellent benefits. I felt maybe this was the beginning of some stability for us, but four months later the problems started again. Joe was involved with drinking, drugs, and very unstable people.

He was upset because I was working, so I ended up quitting my job. I hoped this would improve the situation. It didn't. He would go for days at a time without coming home. When he was home he could care less about the kids or me. I begged him to get help. He refused, saying he didn't know what was wrong, but he had to work it out himself.

Then I found out he was into drugs a lot heavier than I thought – cocaine. Later, after questioning him, he admitted to having an affair. I was destroyed! He said it was still going on and he could not choose between the two of us. I left him a few weeks later. The year was 1987.

The kids and I stayed with my parents. My daughters were 1 and 2 years old. I figured with a little time, he would straighten up and we could return. However, after two months, I was still living with my parents and Joe and I were still not making any progress. My parents were getting very impatient with me. After some problems with them, I moved to my uncle's house.

It took me two more months before I decided I wanted a divorce. Within those two months, my aunt and uncle taught me to drive and I found a job. It was my first step toward independence. The job didn't pay much and I didn't like it, but the money helped. With some financial help from my sister, I was able to retain an attorney, buy a used car, and put a deposit down on an apartment.

Joe was furious when he found out how independent I was becoming. He didn't want the divorce and immediately started causing problems. He refused to pay child support, he began harassing me over the phone, and making kidnapping threats against the girls. There was constantly someone watching my house or following me. The girls suffered most of all. They were confused about the divorce and their dad didn't help matters any. He was very uncooperative and was against everything I tried to do. He wouldn't cooperate with my lawyer or the court.

The stress we were going through was beginning to affect the girls. They were having nightmares and behavioral problems, such as violent temper tantrums, screaming during the night, and severe separation anxiety. I was determined to get them into a more stable environment. I found a much better job.

I soon moved out of our one-bedroom apartment and into a two-bedroom townhouse. Slowly I began to establish myself and we continued dealing with the everyday problems of life. There were work problems, babysitter problems, at times, I had trouble putting food on the table. Of course, there were always lawyer and divorce problems too, but somehow we made it through everything.

My daughters are now teenagers and they are strong girls. We've come a long way. It's all in your attitude and drive. I have found out so much about myself during these past years. I am interested in art, writing, reading, fitness, and nature. I have obtained a degree in business management and have become a certified personal trainer. I am now remarried and have my own business. So many doors have been opened for me. The possibilities now seem endless. I've learned that things happen for a reason and there are always blessings in adversity. You have to take the first step and take control. It's scary but it can be done.

Around the world today many women are victims of domestic violence, and in some cultures it is taught that domestic violence is an expression of love. However, victims of domestic violence often suffer in silence. They may not have anywhere to go. They are afraid of the repercussions of speaking out.

People are sometimes amazed at how many women are victims of molestation and/or physically abuse. The history of these women can keep them from having future healthy relationships because they have not released past hurt.

You have to find a way to deal with past hurts, abusive relationships, and molestation. If you don't release the past, you will bring this bondage into new relationships, and the new relationship will never get off the ground with a legitimate chance of success because of past hurt and pain.

Letting go is challenging because it's a part of our natural instinct to protect ourselves from hurt. Sometimes we think, or project, all men are abusive. They're going to do the same thing to me. The "All men are dogs" type of thinking becomes a self-fulfilling prophesy.

Therefore, you continue to sabotage your present relationship because you have not released yourself from your past relationship. It is still controlling you.

A part of the training in the Champion Woman Seminar is leadership training that gives you the tools and empowers you to release your past, understanding that you can no longer allow yourself to be a prisoner of your past. Being a prisoner of your past hinders you from walking boldly into your future. It makes your present miserable, and it obstructs you from achieving a positive future.

Here are four steps you can take now to release past hurts and begin the healing process:

1). Forgive yourself (don't blame yourself).
2) Forgive those who have caused you pain.
3) Find support.
4) Focus forward.

You have learned resorting to negative reactions to past hurts can prevent you from seeking and adopting positive solutions. In contrast, when you recognize and appropriately express anger or hurt, enormous tension is released and floodgates of emotion are opened.

You experience a sense of peace and well-being as you glimpse the real you. Additionally, as you become more adept at expressing your feelings in an appropriate way as situations arise, you reinforce a greater sense of self. Emotional healing is an ongoing process of change or transformation. The change process should be slow, gentle, and lasting.

In the transformation process, your negative self-concept is replaced by a clear vision of who you are. As your self-knowledge grows and you experience who you truly are, you lay claim to the power you have as a Champion Woman. Above all, you experience a closer personal relationship and union with those who support and love you. In the emotional healing process, you learn you do not have to remain burdened by hurtful emotional baggage, and you learn how to remove the burdens.

Life gives us sunshine and rain. How many of us would prefer to go through a life full of sunshine without experiencing rain? We wouldn't have to listen to the weather report each morning to know what the temperature would be. It would always be sunshine. We could go to the beach, boating, fishing, biking, trekking, or anything we desire because it would always be sunny.

Life gives us sunshine and rain, and if either is deleted we will not grow. Sunny days symbolize good times and little complaints to problems that don't seem to annoy you. Rainy days symbolize tough times, periods in the landscape of life when life itself is a challenge. If we are not careful, we will give up in the midst of tough times.

This is one of most important steps to becoming a Champion Woman, so I want to make sure you understand the importance of releasing whatever hinders you from reaching championship status.

Life might not happen the exact way you would like or how you've planned. There might be pitfalls and detours in the road, but your destiny is still your providence. The desire to become that Champion Woman is still burning inside of you. The fire is hot. Fan the flame. Don't let it quench. Even if life quenches your fire, start over. Collect more wood, make a pile, and start the fire again. You've been derailed a few times, but don't count yourself out. That passion inside of you is your destiny developing.

TCW
DEFINING MOMENTS

What is the most important concept you learned in this chapter?

Why is this concept important to you?

What are three steps you will take to implement this concept into your life?

A CHAMPION WOMAN TESTIMONY

Marsha Freeman

MY CHALLENGE

I had breast cancer not just one time, but two times. I'm a tough cookie. The first time took me by surprise because I was going into surgery thinking I was having a fibroid cyst removed. While I was getting dressed the doctor came in to say, "Sorry, it was cancerous you'll need radiation therapy." Literally, in that second, my life changed.

Up to that point, I was a perfectionist; I thought I had control over everything. I was in control. I'm Marsha Freeman, I'm in control I don't need people to do things for me. Now they had to.

I realized I didn't have control. I found I had to depend on family members and rely on people for advice. No longer was I alone. I began to feel a closer bond with the people around me.

When my younger son found out I had to have chemotherapy, he did not want to return to college in Gainesville. I really didn't want him to change the course of his life, but he insisted.

Once my hair started falling out from the chemo, he very lovingly purchased me a beautiful human hair wig. Most think of having to wear a wig as something negative. However, every time I put it on, I felt I had love right on top of my head. What started as a negative experience turned into a positive experience.

MY LESSON LEARNED

You can't expect to have full control over your life. You have control of about 95 percent of what happens, but we must realize we are human and stuff happens. Those things might alter the course of our lives and if we fight it, we will not be very successful. I had to give in somewhat, but through giving up control I think I gained a lot in terms of what I learned.

I learned not to be such a perfectionist and not to feel I need to have control. Now I'm a happier, more relaxed person and it has given my family time to bond with me.

Part two came about four years later when having another surgery done and a biopsy. The doctor said, "I found some new cancer, since you already had it one time, the lumpectomy and radiation, we recommend you have a double mastectomy."

I fought that for a while, trying to cure myself naturally. It was very stressful and a major, major ordeal. By the time I did decide to do it, I was psychologically ready.

After surgery, it's not a pretty sight but I learned to get through it by visualizing the future and saying to myself, "Things are better in the future." You can deal with the temporary disfiguring or a negative situation you might go through if you can visualize it being better in the future.

MY MESSAGE TO OTHERS

Work to see the positive in negative situations. Going through the reconstruction, that was an ordeal; well, I thought I'll have permanently nice breasts. "I won't have to worry about saggy breasts as some women do. There is a positive to this." I kept seeing things better in the future. That helped me tremendously.

When former New York Mayor Rudy Giuliani was asked how he got through 9/11, he said, "I kept visualizing a better future." Visualize a better future and be patient with yourself because negative people never really accomplish anything but more negativity in their lives.

After the surgery, people asked, "How did you do it?" I said I had some help, but mainly it was a positive attitude. People came to visit me and I was on the couch not in the bed.

The negative part of cancer is out. People kept saying you aren't acting like someone who had surgery yesterday. I put a big smile on my face, because it's all in the positive attitude. I'm not going to be a victim. I'm a survivor.

SECRET #5
REACHING

"Courage is the most important of all the virtues, because without courage you can't practice any other virtue consistently. You can practice any virtue erratically, but nothing consistently without courage."
- *Maya Angelou*

Give it all you've got! It's about passionately pursuing championship status!

So many times in life, you have high aspirations. Aims, objectives, and dreams might sound lofty to some, but deep inside your core you know they are achievable. You've counted the cost, knowing what it will take to reach your goal. You understand that it's not an easy road, but with patience and dedication, you will become a Champion Woman. You've organized your thoughts and your lifestyle in order to change your passion into a reality.

For some reason, though, you're stuck at square one. You know the steps to take, yet you are frozen, immobile. Remember Beatrice the Bagger's story about customer service? You should be your own best customer. However, in order to serve yourself, you must start, or as NIKE says, "Just do it."

I have a friend who offered the following revelation regarding her road to independence to me one day. She told me that during a summer semester in college, since she was working a full-time job, she decided to take one class. This one class met once a month. Her usual school semester contained four classes that she had to attend four days a week. This one class should have been a breeze.

During this summer course, she received a revelation exposing who she was as a procrastinator.

She found that working full-time and taking additional classes were only excuses. The reason she waited until the last possible moment to fulfill her obligations was because she was a Master of Procrastination.

She recalled that the first step to her recovery was admittance. I'm sure that we all can recognize ourselves in at least one of the following identifying marks.

IDENTIFYING

- Do you set unrealistically high standards that make it difficult for you to start a project?
- Do you get lost in details and find it difficult to get a project finished?
- Do you leave projects for the last minute, hoping that time and pressure will motivate you?
- Do you take on so many projects that you can't focus on what needs to be done?
- Do you avoid doing projects because you are angry that you need to do it?
- Do you sometimes avoid a task because you fear doing it?

Having recognized that we share similar identifying marks, we can now focus on the common reasons for procrastination.

PERFECTIONISM

This is probably one of the more common reasons for procrastinating. Perfectionists avoids starting a task because they worry they might fall short of their own high standards.

Perfectionists will become absorbed in the details attempting to control every aspect of the task and ignore moving a project along until the very last minute. They don't have to face their fear of imperfection if the task doesn't get done.

Substitute your thoughts and fears of the project not being perfect with words and thoughts that encourage and motivate you to complete the project. Break the project into manageable stages and components. Take steps daily that will move you closer to the completion of your goals. Set yourself two deadlines: your deadline for when you would like the project to be done and the real deadline. Your goal is to aim at your deadline. Extra time is your reward for completing the project before it is due.

CRISIS MAKER

Crisis Makers believe they cannot get motivated until the very last minute. They upset others because they manufacture a crisis and then solve it at the last minute, making themselves look good in the process. To start a task early is boring to them.

There are those who believe they do their best work at the last minute under pressure. I've learned the quality of one's work is best when it is given the appropriate times spans to be tested, evaluated, and adjusted. Your task is to set earlier deadlines and create rewards for yourself if you are prepared ahead of time.

OVERDOER

Overdoers avoid, but they will never admit it, by taking on other lesser important tasks or projects. They avoid the task by doing more tasks. Their excuse to why they are late is that they just have too many things to do.

It's sometimes hard to identify overdoers because everything is important to them. Get a pencil and paper to prioritize what is really important and what is just busy work.

FANTASIZING

Fantasizers are individuals who are better at dreaming than in dealing with reality. They find it difficult to turn their grandiose thinking into clear concrete plans for action. They can make bosses happy with their great and grand ideas, but later make them frustrated with the lack of results.

Monitor your talk, so you don't bite off more than you can chew. Instead of talking aloud, fantasize only in your head. If you are in a bind, let others know and break down the project in smaller tasks. Set up earlier deadlines than what the real deadline is for the project.

FEAR

This person actually procrastinates because he or she fears doing the task or project at hand. The task has moved these people out of their comfort zones, and the thought of doing it freezes them into immobility.

As soon as you sense fear, take a deep breath, and GO – do not stop. Just do it. By overcoming fear, we conquer and defeat it. Remember 90 percent of what you worry about never happens and the other 10 percent happens, but not as bad as you imagined.

ANGER

Angry people resent having to do the task in the first place. They therefore don't do it out of spite and anger, because they think by doing it they will be giving into the person they are angry at. If they do the task because they have to, it is likely to be done wrong or incompletely.

Work to shift your focus onto the reward of a project well done and away from personalities. Try to see a personal worth or reward in the project that you're doing.

PLEASURE SEEKER

Pleasure seekers delay because there are more fun things to do to fulfill their immediate gratifications. The project can wait. However, rewards come AFTER WORK not BEFORE, just as dessert comes after dinner. If you think that anything besides pleasure is pain, change the word "pain" for the words "temporary inconvenience." Then visualize how good it will make you feel when you have completed the task.

Procrastination is just one of the obstacles or fences you must maneuver on your journey to becoming a Champion Woman. When an obstacle or fence comes your way what do you do? Do you surrender to the barrier? Do you climb over it and continue on your path?

A CEO of a major organization was working after hours as she usually did. All of her employees and co-workers were gone for the weekend. She was waiting on an important call that would solidify a deal that could push her company to one of the top 10 in the nation.

She realized she hadn't eaten all day and knew that because of a diabetic condition that is dangerous, and she must eat at regular intervals. She called ahead to the deli and found they were so busy a delivery would take too long, so she went to pick it up herself.

Paying the clerk, she hurried back to her car, and speeding around the corner, she pulled up to the security gate. Searching around in the car, she realized that in her rush, she forgot her cell phone and the pass card that would enable her to get through the security gate.

Surveying the five-foot fence that surrounded the company, she immediately knew what she had to do. She had to climb the fence. She was beginning to feel weak from lack of food, nerves and the idea that she would have to climb this fence. So she calmly sat in her car, ate half of her sandwich and drank her milk.

Ready for the climb, she took off her jacket, unbuttoned her shirt collar, rolled up her sleeves, took off her stockings and began to scale the fence, the obstacle confronting her. She hadn't climbed a fence since she was a girl. Even though the fence was only five feet tall, it suddenly looked overwhelming but she had to get into her office.

She clenched her teeth and started ascending the fence. Her high heels got caught as her foot slipped when she tried to straddle the fence before descending. Struggling to keep her balance, she slowly moved over the gate and began to climb down.

Just as she stepped into her office, her phone rang and she answered it. She was victorious.

What is your fence? What do you have to climb to reach your goal? What is hindering you from recognizing the Champion Woman you are? Are you a procrastinator? Do you make excuses for your many delays? Are you taking responsibility for your actions?

Be proactive and take the initiative. Participate in the play of your life in which you are the main character. You, Champion Woman, are the leading lady in a major production. Not only are you the main character, you are the scriptwriter, the director, and producer. For you to reach your dream, reach for champion status.

TCW
DEFINING MOMENTS

What is the most important concept you learned in this chapter?

Why is this concept important to you?

What are three steps you will take to implement this concept into your life?

A CHAMPION WOMAN'S TESTIMONY

Wanda Bolton-Davis

MY CHALLENGE

When I told my husband I felt God was calling me into the ministry, he asked me to remember that both of us were raised to believe women were not allowed into the pulpit. As time continued my hunger, thirst, and desire to know God's Word more intimately and heed His call became stronger and stronger. When I mentioned it again to my husband in 1997, he said he did not marry a preacher and he would divorce me if I became one. I put my desire on the back burner.

After my husband accepted a pastoral position in Texas, the family moved there and God began to move in my heart. I mentioned going to seminary school and my husband was supportive, thinking I could use my degree to help his ministry in a variety of ways other than preaching. Besides, I received a scholarship covering the tuition and fees.

After beginning my education in 2001, God began to move quickly. One Sunday morning my husband came to me and acknowledged that women could be preachers. That next Sunday I was licensed. I then graduated, and in the same year was named 2005's Preacher of the Year by Truitt Theological Seminary.

MY LESSON LEARNED

Always remember, God is faithful. Two scriptures come to mind:

John 15:16, "Ye have not chosen me, but I have chosen you, and ordained you, that ye should go and bring forth fruit, and that your fruit should remain: that whatsoever ye shall ask of the Father in my name, he may give it you." – KJV

Proverbs 21: 1, "The king's heart is in the hand of the Lord, as the rivers of water: he turneth it whithersoever he will." – KJV

MY MESSAGE TO OTHERS

Four things:

1) When going through the challenge remember what God told you, no matter how your circumstances appear. Keep your eye on His promise.

2) Know that your destiny is in God's hand and whatsoever He wills shall come to pass.

3) Trust God in the process. "In my life everything happened in His timing: He groomed me, He trained me, and He prepared me." Preparation is the key. Where preparation and opportunity meet therein lies destiny.

4) Wait on God's timing. God does all things well.

SECRET #6

RESPONSIBILITY

"I don't think of myself as a poor deprived ghetto girl who made good. I think of myself as somebody who from an early age knew I was responsible for myself, and I had to make good."
- Oprah Winfrey

Who is responsible for your thoughts? Who is responsible for your actions? Who is responsible for your life? The whole thing of not understanding accountability comes down to understanding responsibility. That is, comprehending the power of every decision you make.

Responsibility requires people to take charge of or be responsible for important matters. They are able to choose for themselves between right and wrong. The consequences can be positive or negative, and it is all within your power. How to take on and manage responsibility is one of the hallmarks of a successful person.

You are responsible for the decisions you make. Every decision is like a type of vehicle. It is a vehicle you are entering. The question to ask before you choose to enter the vehicle is, will this vehicle transport me to my desired future to reach champion status?

Every day we are presented with ideas, choices, opportunities and decisions that must be scrutinized. If decisions are a vehicle, a Champion Woman does not ride in just anyone's vehicle. Many vehicles look nice on the outside, but on the inside they might not possess the capacity to enable you to reach your goals.

For example, a BMW looks nice if what you want to do is drive around town, but if you wanted to race in the Daytona 500, it would not be sufficient. You must scrutinize the process to decide its capability and capacity. You scrutinize the vehicle based on what your goals are.

People present you with vehicles all the time. They could be relationships, a job, a business decision or a religious decision. Ultimately, it is up to you to take the responsibility to scrutinize the vehicle before you make the decision. We climb into vehicles every day, but they might not take us to our desired destination. Remember, every vehicle will drive you towards or away from your goal to becoming a Champion Woman.

This might be a time to evaluate the types of vehicles you are currently riding in. God created you to be a Champion Woman, and in doing so He equipped you with the gifts and tools necessary to become a Champion Woman. These innate gifts and talents do not come without responsibility.

What is it that makes you valuable? Each of us has gifts and talents that make us unique and gives us our value. They are our assets. So often becoming a Champion Woman and successful is delayed because we focus on our deficiencies rather than our assets. People tend to focus on each other's deficiencies and weaknesses as opposed to their strengths. Most of all, you cannot depend on others to tell you what your assets are.

Recognize you do have the power, the power to move you toward your destiny. You have to take responsibility to do what is required to be successful. It's about eliminating excuses. It's not always people who are less qualified getting promoted over you. Perhaps they are being promoted because their attitudes are better. Do they get to work on time? Do they perform the job the way the boss wants them to? Are they taking responsibility for their own actions?

The entire idea is to own it. You have the power --- it's up to YOU. A large part of your destiny and success is being psychologically aware that you have the power and capability to take the actions and do what is required. You want to be a successful entrepreneur, a mother, a wife; whatever your goal, you have to recognize and understand that you have to personally take the actions.

Your responsibility is foremost to yourself and it is threefold. Let's look at it in 3-D: Discovery, Develop and Dispersed.

DISCOVERY

First you must take the responsibility to discover your innate and learned gifts and talents. Identifying your strengths is a journey of self-exploration, one that must be done with candidness and honesty.

A talent or gift might be something as seemingly insignificant as being a good listener or noticing the good things about others and complimenting them. Also, this is not just about things you like to do but identifying what you really do well. For example, some people like to sing but it is clear to everyone within earshot that singing is not one of their gifts or talents.

What are three things that you do extremely well?
    a.
    b.
    c.

What are three things that others have consistently commented you do well or complimented you on?
 a.
 b.
 c.

DEVELOP

After you have taken the journey of *discovery* and self-exploration, the second step is to *develop* your gifts and talents. Development is having a systematic plan for cultivating your gifts and talents so you can maximize your full potential and obtain Champion Power.

It is not a one-time step or an overnight process. It is a lifetime commitment to doing something every day to make yourself better. You are taking a first step by reading this book and attending the Champion Woman seminars.

There are components to Champion Power that are vital to self development. The end goal of self-development is about becoming an expert and developing the strengths you have identified during your discovery period. You must cultivate your discovered talents and gifts so you maximize your potential.

In the development process you are developing Champion Power. *Champion Power* is the ability and the capacity to do. We are talking about maximum power. We want our life operating at its full potential.

Champion Power is getting the four key cylinders of your life operating at maximum strength and in harmony.

The first power is *intellectual power*, which is getting the education and training you need to develop your skills, further your goals and maximize your potential.

The second power is b*orrowed power,* which is about having mentors and surrounding yourself with individuals who will allow you to borrow their wisdom, expertise and guidance.

The third is a *physical power* which is about fitness and taking care of the body. It is important that you have the health and physical strength to move in your journey as a Champion Woman.

The fourth and foundational power is s*piritual* which is about the acknowledgement and interdependence on the highest power, God. It is a power that gives you the faith to believe in yourself, hope to believe in tomorrow, and the strength to overcome all human obstacles.

Here's the thing: You have discovered and are developing your gifts and talents. But what good are these gifts if you do not share them with others? They must be *dispersed* into the world.

DISPERSING

Dispersing is about giving of the gifts you have been blessed with. You have identified and cultivated them, now how are you using them?

The gift is the seed and the world is the fertile ground. The world is not in need of more gifted and talented people, there is not a dearth of talent or assets. In our world today, the communities we live in, and our families there is the issue of a selfish reluctance and a fear to share. Part of it is we live in the "me" culture and consider most other people "them". Anyone who has become a true champion possessing Champion Power did so with the help of others. You cannot achieve Champion Power by yourself. There is a need of those who would disperse their gifts in such a way that it enriches humanity.

Recognizing motivating factors in your lives helps keep you on track. Your self-descriptions are confident and optimistic. Even though self-assessments can be difficult, you are empowered by altering your paradigms and expanding your horizons. Your past may be full of mistakes and regrettable decisions, but you are changing the next chapter of your story by burying the negative past and taking responsibility in creating a brighter and positive future.

Your thought process is turning into positive beliefs by respecting yourself and demanding respect from others. You daily let go of baggage that, if given room to cultivate, will stagnant your growth. You are pursuing your dreams, your passions and are taking full responsibility for your actions by being accountable. Now it's time to reap your reward, the reward of maximizing your potential by reaching championship status.

TCW
DEFINING MOMENTS

What is the most important concept you learned in this chapter?

Why is this concept important to you?

What are three steps you will take to implement this concept into your life?

A CHAMPION WOMAN TESTIMONY

Helen King

MY CHALLENGE

When told I could not have a child, I felt stagnant and my life was an emotional landslide. I was constantly thinking, "Why is this happening to me?" I set goals for myself and achieved them, but I couldn't have the thing I wanted most: a child. During my season of wanting, almost anything someone said to me would stab a hole in my heart.

Seven years and eight months, I waited. One of my most difficult struggles was the reaction of others. It did not matter the location or caliber of people. It happened in the pews at church, the teacher's lounge, the hair salon, as well as family reunions. I had several people look me in the eye and ask, "So, do you even want to have kids? And if so, why are you waiting so long to start a family?" It appeared the more evasive I was the deeper they delved, not realizing the pain their questions inflicted upon me.

Looking at me from the outside I seemed fine, but inside everything was out of place. On the outside, I always looked like I had it all together. Inside, I was crying silent tears. Family, friends, and well wishers repeatedly said, "Just relax," or asked, "Have we considered adoption?" I constantly prayed and asked God for help.

MY LESSON LEARNED

The lesson I learned from this experience was to trust God. God led me to start a ministry called Totally Relinquishing Unto Our Savior Today and Tomorrow

(T.R.U.S.T.). I minister to women going through infertility issues. I realized women facing the challenges of infertility need to talk about it to learn to heal.

It is my belief that one cannot conquer what one is not willing to face. Through prayer and fasting, God allowed me to minister to others during my season of waiting. It wasn't easy, but it was during those times that my prayer life became stronger. I would go to God in prayer with my raw feelings and lay them all before him. It was at those times that I felt validated because God didn't judge me. God listened and comforted me. It was during this season that I learned my favorite scripture, Proverbs 3: 5-6, "Trust in the Lord with all your heart and lean not on your own understanding. In all your ways acknowledge Him and He shall direct your path." (KJV)

MY MESSAGE TO OTHERS

When someone is going through a season of waiting: Lend a listening ear. Many ask me why I continue to hold T.R.U.S.T. meetings when I have conceived and now have my miracle baby. My answer is always the same: "I will always remember. I will never forget my season of waiting." I dedicate my life to encouraging as many women as I can.

I want others to understand that they are not alone.

SECRET #7

REWARD

"I believe in me more than anything in this world."
- *Wilma Rudolph*

Chorus:

All I ever wanted was to be a superstar,
Sometimes I look,
I can't believe that I have come this far.
They said I'd never make it,
They always said I would never amount to no good.
But if I can do it,
You can do it,
Just follow your heart,
And don't let anybody try and tear your dreams apart.
You'll be a superstar...

Artist: Gemma Fox **Album:** Messy **Title:** Superstar

  Edna did it. She plotted and stuck to her course, overcame obstacles, and persisted even when she wanted to give up. She took full advantage of her possibilities to become a Champion Woman. Edna refused to be stuck in a past of misfortune and missed opportunities. She finally realized that she was more than her previous history and wanted to create a new future. A prospect filled with hope, satisfaction, anticipation of respect, and admiration.
  Edna accomplished all her expectations and more. When she focused on what lies ahead of her, learning from what had happened previously but not dwelling on it, she

was able to bring the mental image of what she expected into fruition. It was challenging. Some days it seemed impossible. Edna was convinced with faith and courage that what was to occur in her life would deliver contentment of mind, body, and soul.

Edna rejected flawed principles. She regularly examined her thinking, making sure she put a positive spin on negative thoughts. She acquired the skill of recognizing that everyone has their own paradigms. It's not always a right or wrong concept. She is now able to shift her own personal perceptions by valuing the ideas of others.

Edna programmed, or trained, herself to live one day at a time, concentrating on one area at a time. First, she transformed her mind to believe she was who she chose to be. She defined herself. She didn't allow others to characterize her. She named herself. The name she chose is EDNA (written as an acronym): **E**ncourager (giving others and herself hope, confidence or courage), **D**efiant (challenging aggressively; tending to confront and challenge), **N**urturing (encouraging others to grow, develop, thrive and be successful), and **A**chiever (successful and motivated person).

Beatrice achieved redefining herself and her job by going the extra mile in delivering customer service. She listened to wise counsel, deciding how to benefit not only her, but also others she encountered. She surrounded herself with positive, supportive people she could depend on to give helpful advice and feedback.

Beatrice understood what Charles Swindoll meant when he stressed the importance of attitude. She could have complained and whined when senior management informed employees of the possibility of layoffs. She realized that administration had invested a lot into their staff over the years and thought their individual input would be important. Beatrice became aware that she was a valuable asset to the establishment, and as a precious commodity, she must invest in herself.

Beatrice managed the strain of impending job loss by emphasizing her importance. She began to respect herself mentally by visualizing the positive benefits her heartening words would have on the customers, co-workers, supervisors, and herself. She committed to the process daily. The homework assignment had been for one day, but Beatrice continued to invest her time and resources into bringing a measure of joy to others daily.

Monique Rider accomplished championship status. She took control of her script, changing the set location and characters to allow the end of her story to conform to her liking. You can attain it. You can dream your dreams and awaken to a reality that exceeds all your expectations. You can enjoy the fruits of your labor, Champion Woman.

Monique could have easily thrown in the towel. For years, she accepted what fate had given her. Monique demanded a relationship where each person dealt with the other at their highest level. She was tired of living in the basement. She wanted to breathe the rich air of socially and culturally diverse experiences. Monique beat the odds by eventually taking her script back. She was in charge of the edits, removing offensive actions from publication.

Monique released the bondage of her past by acknowledging the importance of her feelings. She expressed her value as a woman, wife, and mother. She experienced the sorrow of separation, knowing that in her case, she had to detach herself from an abusive relationship in order to progress.

Edna, Monique, and Beatrice did it – and so can you. Championship status is about maximizing your potential, your talents, and your gifts. The payoff is discovering your strengths and developing them. The reward is being able to experience success.

Your recompense is to become a positive thinker; you now think of yourself as regal. You absolutely, without a doubt, know that you are royalty. Men are now dealing with you as a monarch's patronage, at your highest level. You have relationships and fulfilling associations as your compensation. The prize is all the benefit of the Champion Power secrets.

Being responsible and accountable in all areas and dimensions of your life has significant benefits and rewards. You are discovering, developing, and dispersing your God-given talents and gifts. The vehicles you scrutinized and choose keep you from being repeatedly in relationships that don't go anywhere. Now your relationships enhance and fulfill you. You are a whole woman.

The woman who thinks, talks and walks like a winner usually is a winner. That is you, Champion Woman. You maintain your composure in stressful situations. You radiate self-assurance and project confidence in every area of your life. What secret do you hold? You hold the secret of knowing who you are. You don't rely on others to define you. You label yourself: gifted, confident, powerful, positive, and intelligent. That's you! You are assured in yourself and the gifts that you have. Others see the champion in you and strive to be like you. You are the role model your children, co-workers, and associates endeavor to follow.

You now possess the secrets. The seven secrets of becoming a Champion Woman are in your grasp. Take a leap of faith and plunge into your greatness. You are the "Phenomenal Woman" Maya Angelou wrote about in her poem.

Phenomenal Woman

Pretty women wonder where my secret lies.
I'm not cute or built to suit a fashion model's size
But when I start to tell them,
They think I'm telling lies.
I say,
It's in the reach of my arms
The span of my hips,
The stride of my step,
The curl of my lips.
I'm a woman
Phenomenally.
Phenomenal woman,
That's me.

I walk into a room
Just as cool as you please,
And to a man,
The fellows stand or
Fall down on their knees.
Then they swarm around me,
A hive of honey bees.
I say,
It's the fire in my eyes,
And the flash of my teeth,
The swing in my waist,
And the joy in my feet.
I'm a woman
Phenomenally.
Phenomenal woman,
That's me.

Men themselves have wondered
What they see in me.

They try so much
But they can't touch
My inner mystery.
When I try to show them
They say they still can't see.
I say,
It's in the arch of my back,
The sun of my smile,
The ride of my breasts,
The grace of my style.
I'm a woman

Phenomenally.
Phenomenal woman,
That's me.

Now you understand
Just why my head's not bowed.
I don't shout or jump about
Or have to talk real loud.
When you see me passing
It ought to make you proud.
I say,
It's in the click of my heels,
The bend of my hair,
the palm of my hand,
The need of my care,
'Cause I'm a woman
Phenomenally.
Phenomenal woman,
That's me.

- Maya Angelou
Phenomenal – Champion Woman, that's you.

TCW
DEFINING MOMENTS

What is the most important concept you learned in this chapter?

Why is this concept important to you?

What are three steps you will take to implement this concept into your life?

A CHAMPION WOMAN TESTIMONY

Linda Scott

MY CHALLENGE

My first-born child died at the age of 24. It was the hardest thing I ever faced. My daughter was in good health and recently gave birth to a baby boy who was less than a year old.

Prior to losing my only daughter I had never gone through a challenge that I couldn't overcome. We were very close, very connected with each other and were just on our way to see each other when I received the news of her death. Even though it's been almost 11 years, it seems like it was just yesterday.

We all know that we will pass from this journey of life, yet we as parents, never expect to lose one of our children before we depart this world. Life tends to teach us that the elderly are to depart before the children.

My husband and I became legal guardians over our 9-month-old grandson. We have always been a close-knit family, showing our love in action not just words. We are truly there for one another. Had it not been for the love and encouragement of my family, I could not have dealt with the pain that I sometimes continually feel, even today.

A major challenge was learning to readjust my life after losing her. Since she and I were extremely close, this challenge is ongoing.

MY LESSON LEARNED

From this experience, I've learned that you don't know what tomorrow holds so, please, live life to the fullest every day. This is the day the Lord has made. Rejoice and be happy in it! Enjoy it! Any dreams you might have, go after them. Remember: This is who you are, this is what you want, and this is who you want to be. Life is too short to take one minute for granted.
As time passed, I realized I found comfort in knowing that my daughter knew she was loved and cherished. The last time I spoke with her, I told her that I loved her. Today I never let my children leave without saying I love them.
When I asked God why my daughter was taken from me leaving her son motherless, God answered by giving me more daughters, young ladies to care for. In 2006, I started a company that guides young women in developing healthy self-esteem in order to meet the challenges of life and live it to the fullest.

MY MESSAGE TO OTHERS

In the past, we had "Big Mommas" who taught us how to behave as ladies. Today the Big Mommas are getting younger and younger with little time to teach young ladies what it means to truly be a woman of character. They themselves haven't been taught how to operate to their highest possibility.
My message to others is to go back to yesterday, when respect for yourself and others was something everyone tried to practice. Open up, reach out, and lend a hand. As corny as that sound, just lend a hand to a youngster. It could take two minutes of your time to reach out and let someone in your life.

A CHAMPION WOMAN TESTIMONY

Pearl M. Davis

MY CHALLENGE

I was raised by born-again Christians who lived within the Bible Belt of South Florida. My parents married at a young age and built a family of 11 children. They defined their roles as partners, parents, and Christians. I never witnessed an argument or display of unloving behavior from either of them toward each other or any of us. Don't misunderstand me – we had to be and were disciplined. However, we always knew why and eventually it felt like love.

At the age of 16, I became friends with a young man who seven years later asked for my hand in marriage. My father nearly refused to agree to the marriage. I did not understand his reasons at the time. My mother, the nurturing one, understood my desires and reluctantly agreed to allow me to marry. I could not hold a conversation with my father about my wedding or marriage. Discussions surrounding the wedding would encourage my father to leave the room.

On my wedding day, I was prepared to have my older brother give me away. My father came home from work as we were getting dressed to go to the church. The entire wedding party was moving about the family home. He walked to his bedroom and remained until we were preparing to leave. He came out dressed to give me away, and that he did.

Married life was wonderful, first child born 18 months later, running my household and working full-time. Less than a year later things became shaky. I was not able to talk to anyone because I was proving to my father that my husband was worthy.

As the years passed, instability became stronger and unity suffered a continued breakdown. About nine years into the marriage, I personally surrendered and accepted that I'd made a huge mistake. At this point, God blessed us with another child. Just as my mom did, I take parenting serious. I feel privileged to have been chosen twice to produce and develop children in a manner pleasing to God. That excitement held things together for as long as it could. Eventually, I was back at square one, surrendering to failure.

Throughout my life and marriage, I knew my family frowned upon divorce. I'd heard so many stories and statistics regarding the hardship of a single mother and the rise in that number within society. As much as it saddened me, it also helped me see that it could be acceptable, understandable, and normal.

After more than 18 years of marriage with children ages 17 and 7, I asked for a divorce. Although I had my freedom and could spread my wings, I went into this lifestyle with boxing gloves ready to face the following fears:

- Lack of support from ex-husband with the development of children.
- Resentment and anger from children for removing their father from the home.
- Potential financial hardship due to reduced income.
- Likelihood of not being available to engage in another meaningful relationship for many years.
- Acceptance of failure at one of the greatest life changing decisions I'd ever made.

MY LESSON LEARNED

I created my game plan and remained focused. The plan would change more often than I was accustomed to, but I didn't mind changing my course of action. Eventually, I realized I actually had total control of my destiny! That's when the game changed! All of those fears were turned around and gave a whole new meaning.

- Lack of support from ex-husband turned into, "**When is the next ball game? I want to be there.**"
- Resentment from children turned into "**Mom, I love you so much for all that you do for me. I see the sacrifices you make and it doesn't bother you at all. I don't question your love for me.**"
- Potential financial hardship turned into **financial stability.**
- Likelihood of not being available to engage in a meaningful relationship turned into, **engaging in healthier, more meaningful relationships.**
- Acceptance of failure changed to **independent success.**

The real lesson in all of this is to realize that my attitude toward my circumstances changed a predictable outcome to an extraordinary success. I believe in God and I believe in me.

MY MESSAGE TO OTHERS

Look for the positive in negative situations. Listen to your parents, dearest friends, and other mentors who give you advice about decisions surrounding your future.

Plan, plan, plan! Don't be discouraged if you have to change the plan. Some plans are short-term with long-term benefits. Just change the plan and work it. The better you plan, the stronger you are when facing hurdles. Your plan helps you to see what might occur. Draw strength from disappointments. Brush yourself off and try a different approach. Do not fail to try and try again.

Take the time to raise your children. Find resources to support your mission with their personal development. Guide them in seeing the big picture while they are small. Encourage them to aim for the gold and develop them to do it independently. Let no man, woman, organization, or thing take precedence over your responsibility to love, provide, and protect your children.

Live life with the intent to enjoy every day God has granted you. Pray with a plan in mind.

A CHAMPION WOMAN TESTIMONY

Gloria Ortiz

MY CHALLENGE

My challenge in life was that of acceptance. There are women who suffer with a lack of self-esteem, and I was one of them. We are confronted with insecurity about our outward appearance. Although I grew up in a loving, two-parent home and was encouraged, with my parents nurturing me to the best of their ability, insecurity still plagued me. Little girls are inundated by the pillage of mass media that portrays beauty as thin, blond-haired, and blue-eyed. That did not look like me. Instead, I saw ethnic races negatively portrayed. I am sure other girls just like me compared themselves to this media version.

MY LESSON LEARNED

Through searching God's word, I learned I am beautiful and wonderfully made. I am one of a kind. God created us all just as we are and He loves us, so we must love ourselves inside and out. The King James Version of the Bible states in Psalm 139 verse 14, "I will praise thee, for I am fearfully and wonderfully made; marvelous are thy works; and that my soul knoweth right well."

MY MESSAGE TO OTHERS

Love yourself. Seek God to comfort you and help you to see yourself as He created you. God's light is bright and through His Love, others will see you as He does, inwardly. Reflect on your beauty within and it will show without. Let your light shine.

A CHAMPION WOMAN TESTIMONY

Sharon Dunn

MY CHALLENGE

My husband died 15 years ago, when my boys were 10 and 3. It's hard raising kids alone, especially when problems arise. When my eldest son was 16 years old, he developed chronic debilitating back pain which, after tests, was diagnosed as scoliosis, or curvature of the spine. We were told that spinal fusion was a strong possibility. After reading up on spinal fusion, I was horrified. Considered one of the most dangerous and painful surgeries today, fusion complications can occasionally cause paralysis, and even death. More commonly, it creates more pain and repeat operations. Recovery can take months.

I was terrified for my son. I knew there had to be something more progressive than an outdated surgery that had been around for almost 100 years. I relentlessly searched daily on the Internet, in bookstores, the library, and on the phone with scoliosis specialists from as far away as Spain. I took my son to see orthopedic specialists in numerous states, but no one could help.

In the meantime, my son's pain was getting much worse. Now a collegiate, his back pain became disabling. His doctor's solution was to prescribe painkillers that are more powerful. My son told me the painkillers didn't take away the pain. Instead, they numbed everything, including his brain.

Desperate, I flew from Canada where I lived to California, where my son was living, to help him. I didn't know what I was going to do, but I vowed not to leave him until the problem was solved. I was shocked to see that he was in worse shape than I thought. In dire pain, he could barely sit straight. We saw another specialist, again to no avail.

One morning as I was doing another deep search, I came across a site touting a scoliosis brace for adults. This was something new, although I was told consistently there was no such thing. I started making calls and by the end of that very day, spoke with the inventor of the Spinecor brace, Dr. Charles Hilaire Rivard, an orthopedic surgeon in Montreal. He confidently told me that the brace would help my son. I cried with relief.

I was worried again when I found out the brace was not supported by the medical profession. **That's why I had never heard of it.** A journalist by profession, I was skeptical, but not as skeptical as my son. He finally agreed and was fitted with the brace by a chiropractor in California who Dr. Rivard trained. I hoped and prayed that this unrecognized brace would work.

Within a couple of days, my son was pleasantly surprised to report that his back pain was declining – dramatically. Within two months the pain that plagued him for years was gone. Today, almost four years later, he still has no back pain.

Three years ago, I wrote an article for MacLeans Magazine called "Amazing Brace." It was about my journey to find help for my son. I wrote it to help others. I couldn't stand to think that other scoliosis sufferers, young and old, were desperate to find help, but no one was telling them about this great brace that had helped my son so much. I wanted to change that.

Because of my story, I've received hundreds of letters from people around the world desperate for help with nowhere to turn. What started as a terrible journey for me and my son turned out to be one of the most rewarding experiences of my life. Many of the people who have written have subsequently had their children or themselves fitted with the brace. I still receive thank-you letters from so many who have been helped. Just today, I received two more letters – one from the husband of a 63-year-old scoliosis sufferer in bad pain needing help and another from a mother whose daughter is being treated successfully by Dr. Rivard.

MY LESSON LEARNED

The main lesson here is not only does "persistence pay off," but more than that, sometimes you have to buck the system. It's very difficult to have doctor after doctor tell you "braces don't work" and go ahead with it anyway. I did my research. I looked at my son's suffering and made a call. It turned out to be the right one. After my son's great success with the brace, I called a number of surgeons we had seen to let them know how my son had been helped, so they could pass information to other patients who needed help. Not one of the surgeons called me back. Don't get me wrong; I am a big believer in the medical profession, but I learned doctors are human, too. They aren't God, and sometimes we have to look deeper for the answer. All my life, I've been told that I'm too aggressive, too independent, and too driven. Thank God. It has finally paid off.

MY MESSAGE TO OTHERS

I now have a scoliosis blog where I post letters from people who need help, or who have success stories from the Spinecor brace. You can access it from **sharondunn.com**.
My experience has confirmed what I always knew. There is always an answer if you keep searching, and don't

take no for an answer. Don't forget to think outside the box and believe you can make a difference.

A CHAMPION WOMAN TESTIMONY

Teri Williams

MY CHALLENGE

One would think being a high school art teacher is a peaceful, cool job, but the tragedy that struck one of my students was anything but peaceful. It was 10 years ago but I remember it like it was yesterday.

This young man, in his sophomore year, came from a well-to-do family who went out of the country on business. Leaving their responsible son with enough money to cover his expenses while they were away, he took the money and bought a gun. His family returned to find out that their son had committed suicide. In his suicide note he stated, "Tell them I'm not gay."

This devastating occurrence changed the course of my life. I wished I could have done something to help that child. I realized I couldn't stand by and just teach I had to take action. I had to challenge myself, and others, to build holistic and creative approaches to violence prevention.

MY LESSON LEARNED

I learned we have to be willing to step out of our comfort zones. I learned to be an advocate of discussion and to utilize clear, honest communication with my students so they will become champions instead of victims.

MY MESSAGE TO OTHERS

Become an agent of action who helps empower and transform others. Know that you have choices. You can either curl up in a ball of rage and scream, or be an agent of action doing something about your circumstance or the circumstances of others. Determine what an agent of action looks like to you. What does that mean to you? Even if you've chosen poorly at one point, it doesn't mean it's over. Allow it to become an opportunity to do something magnificent in your life and the lives of others.

A CHAMPION WOMAN TESTIMONY

Renee Brown

MY CHALLENGE

At age 25, a combination of things occurred that plummeted me into a deep depression. I was totally dissatisfied with my career. A love interest and paying attention to my outward beauty helped mask my dissatisfaction. Like many women, I looked to the outside appearance for acceptance and feelings of self-worth. Suddenly, I was diagnosed with a severe case of chicken pox, which left me marked and feeling ugly.

Instead of talking about how I felt, I internalized my feelings and began to turn inward on myself. My personality shifted from being outgoing and positive to secluded and withdrawn. I didn't care about my understanding and patient man. Within three months, I resigned from my job, left town, moved home to Florida, leaving my man and everything behind. It was just another way of evading the problem.

I felt numb. After doctor's evaluations and pumping me up with medication, it was like God heard my silent call for help and knew just what I needed. I happened upon a previous acquaintance who is a psychologist. I felt God put her in my path.

I began to pray. God put it in my heart that my healing would occur through a spiritual route. I stopped taking all medications.

Sixteen years later, I'm married to the man who patiently waited for me and we have two sons. Now helping others, my husband and I are over the Marital Counseling Center (MCC) at our house of worship.

MY LESSON LEARNED

Find someone to talk over your problems and feelings. If you cannot find a person you can trust, talk to God. Communication is always the key. Most of my suffering came from not talking about my feelings and internalizing how I felt.

MY MESSAGE TO OTHERS

Scott Hamilton, Olympic gold medal figure skater, wrote a book called *"The Great Eight: How to Be Happy Even When You Have Every Reason to Be Miserable,"* which speaks about God's Scheduled Opportunity (GSO). Hamilton writes, "When you start looking at everything that happens in your life as a God Scheduled Opportunity, it is amazing how it not only brightens your outlook, but how it infuses you with a greater sense of purpose, direction, and confidence." (p. 24)

Not every problem we encounter is "from the devil." Some are simply GSO moments. These GSO moments are hidden blessings, times in our life to fine tune who we are. They are opportunities to use ourselves in a manner that is pleasing to God and His kingdom. They present us with challenges that will inevitably benefit us; make us better people.

A CHAMPION WOMAN TESTIMONY

Amanda Wright

MY CHALLENGE

My biggest challenge was conquering my disbelief in God and the hate I carried in my heart. I had given up on my life. I had no faith. I saw no way out, and I felt poor in spirit.

I was young, about 15 or 16, when I saw my stepfather commit a heinous crime against my family members. He killed my mother and brother then shot me. After losing them, a great spirit of fear came upon me. I was afraid. I didn't want to live. I felt it wasn't fair for me to eat or remain alive.

My mouth and my attitude started the problems in my home. I insinuated something bad between my stepfather and my mother. The house was without peace. Back then, my brother and I felt like it was our way or no way. I didn't know peace should be in the home, that we should be as one and love each other. I didn't see that because he was not my father. I did not respect him and I thought he was phony.

MY LESSON LEARNED

I overcame hate and love was restored in me. I changed because I gave God a chance to show Himself in my life. I surrendered my life and received salvation. I read the Bible and got to know God for myself. I overcame the hate in my heart and replaced it with peace, love, and the belief that there is a God and He is Almighty.

I learned how to stay humble and God has greatly bridled my tongue. I look at things in a different perspective now. I have a great outlook on even the worst things. God helped me conquer a suicidal spirit.

I learned to always believe in myself and always believe God will work it out. Although you have a strong belief in yourself, it is not good to be overconfident because anything can happen. That is why it is important to believe God has a purpose for you and your life. There is a greatness that lies ahead of you. I learned to be humble to love and to forgive. Definitely, I really learned to forgive despite circumstances.

MY MESSAGE TO OTHERS

My message to and for others who are on life's battlefield is fight to the end and never give up. No matter what thorns or obstacles might come your way, always keep moving. Sometimes we don't have time to fall down and get up to brush our knees off. No, sometimes we must run with our knees dirty and skinned up, so we can see where we came from. You will remember the obstacle you overcame once you observe your survival wounds. That alone will keep you humble while you strive for more and learn to receive.

If God did it for me He will do it for everyone. Believe me; I was on the verge of suicide.

A TALE TO REMEMBER

Do you remember the children's story, "The Three Little Pigs?" When our parents, teachers, or guardians read this story with expression or feeling and we closed our eyes, we could imagine that this tale had a realistic edge to it. We could almost feel the hot breath of the Big Bad Wolf as he huffed and puffed on each occasion. Fear evoked action from the pigs. Author Bruno Bettelheim in the book, *The Uses of Enchantment, the Meaning and Importance of Fairy Tales*, writes, "'The Three Little Pigs' teaches the nursery-age child in a most enjoyable and dramatic form that we must not be lazy and take things easy, for if we do, we may perish. Intelligent planning and foresight combined with hard labor will make us victorious over even our most ferocious enemy – the wolf!"

In the beginning of this fairy tale, each pig was sent out by their mother to seek fame and fortune – or in other words to achieve their individual dream and goal. Now if it were us in this story, we would be sent out in the world to become Champion Women.

We as the little pigs must leave our comfort zone and face certain fears in life. In this story, it just so happens that the fears are all found the character of the Big Bad Wolf. In real life, the wolf is not subject to stay in one form, but can come in a variety of appearances, past hurts and wounds, loveless relationships, and low self-esteem.

With our goal in view, we are excited at this venture, and eager to start our journey of turning the world upside down as we become Champion Women. Each of us has a style or individual road map that we wish to follow. Even though each reader of this book has a championship goal to accomplish, we each will decide independently what route to take.

Will you chart your course and follow the example of the first little pig who thoughtlessly threw together a house of straw, or will you tag along with the middle pig using sticks to quickly and effortlessly attempt to reach your goal? The first pig sought instant gratification, throwing some straw on the ground and considering it shelter. In this microwave society, we have to be so careful not to let our impatience rule us.

We have been conditioned almost since birth to expect things quickly. There was a time when getting a manicure was a time of relaxation. Pour a little warm water in a bowl, squeeze in a little Palmolive and soak for a while. This was after the fingernails had been clipped and filed. One hand would soak, while the other hand casually flipped through a magazine. Then after pushing back the cuticle, a base coat would be applied, then the chosen color and then a top coat. At least 10 minutes between coats was an acceptable time. Now, if you get a manicure, you get the quick drying polish or you go to the nail salon in the mall to get nails that don't need to be clipped or filed or polished until you go back again a few weeks later.

Immediate gratification can be your way of life, if you don't monitor your time tolerance. On our quest to reach our goals there is no quick fix to obtaining championship status.

Are you putting a little thought into the process, counting the costs and then letting the fear of responsibility immobilize us? Will you tag along with the middle pig using sticks to quickly and effortlessly try to reach your goal? The middle pig wasn't a great step up from the first pig. He had a little control over his impatience, but didn't count the cost. His route didn't take much planning or insight. He only thought of the here and now and not down the road. When you decided to become a Champion Woman, short-term and long-term goals were put in place.

If obtaining a college education is your goal but you work more than 40 hours a week and take care of a family, it would be more manageable to take a few classes a semester than try to schedule a full load. Count the cost. You would have your regular duties as employee, wife, and mother and have added the duty of student. Each comes with high expectations. Make each obligation controllable.

Don't overextend yourself by picking up too many sticks at once, trying to force them into the shape of a home. Plan your course. Have a back-up route. You can be successful at any endeavor you choose, but planning and patience is necessary.

The third pig realized he had a responsibility not only to himself, but also to his family to become successful. He was accountable to himself, his mother, his family, and community. Accountability empowers challenges us; it creates conflict in our mind. It demands that we recondition the way we think and behave. It would have been easy for him to act as his siblings had, taking the uncomplicated road. He put thought into the process. He realized as we do that victorious accomplishments don't come over night. They don't come trouble-free or effortless. Achieving your dreams takes dedication, endurance, and patience.

KNOWLEDGE FOR YOU

DIETARY GUIDELINES

Following a healthy diet permits you to alleviate stress, while fueling your mind and body. The **dietary guidelines** in the Pyramid consist of fruits, vegetables, whole grains and meats. At the 2,000-calorie level, here's what the guidelines suggest.

- **Fruit Group:** should provide four daily servings, or 2 cups.
- **Vegetable Group:** should provide servings, or 2.5 cups.
- **Grain Group:** should provide 6 ounce-equivalents (1 ounce-equivalent means serving), half of which should be whole grains.
- **Meat and Beans Group:** should provide 5.5 ounce-equivalents or servings.
- **Milk Group:** should provide 3 cups/servings.
- **Oils:** should provide 24g or 6 teaspoons.
- **Discretionary Calories:** These are the remaining amount of calories in each calorie level after nutrient-dense foods have been chosen. Up to 267 calories can be consumed in solid fats or added sugars if the other requirements have been met.

The Pyramid does not spell this out because 2,000 calories is not appropriate for everyone. Instead, the color bands represent a visual clue about what proportion of our diet these foods should form.

Surround yourselves with positive, supportive people you can depend on to give you helpful advice and feedback.

DOMESTIC VIOLENCE

Victims of domestic violence and abuse are not able to live quality lives until they release themselves of past hurts and pain.

Domestic Violence Statistics:

- **A woman is beaten every 15 seconds.** *(Uniform Crime Reports, Federal Bureau of Investigation, 1991)*

- **The American Medical Association now estimates that almost 4 million women are victims of severe assaults by boyfriends and husbands each year, and about one in four women is likely to be abused by a partner in her lifetime.** *(Sarah Glazer, "Violence Against Women," CQ Researcher, Congressional Quarterly, Inc., Vol. 3 No.8, February 1993, p. 171)*

- **Women are more often victims of domestic violence than victims of burglary, mugging, or other physical crimes combined.** *("First Comprehensive National Health Survey of American Women," Commonwealth Fund, July 1993)*

- **Experts suggest domestic elder abuse is perhaps the most underreported crime. Older adults are reluctant to report abuse because they are ashamed to admit that their spouse or children have mistreated them. Most fear retaliation or dread institutionalization if they are removed** from the care of the abuser. In addition, cognitive and physical impairments may make it impossible for some elderly individuals to report their abuse. *(Payne, B.K. Crime and Elder Abuse: An Integrated Perspective, Springfield, IL: Charles C. Thomas, 2000)*

- **In 1999, 470,702 cases of abuse and neglect were reported to adult protective services throughout the United States. This is a 62 percent increase since 1996.***(National Clearinghouse on Abuse in Later Life, 2001)*

- **A study of 257 older women ages 50-79 found that 32 percent experienced physical violence in their relationships within the past year.** *(Mouton, 1999)*

- **In almost 90 percent of the elder abuse and neglect incidents with a known perpetrator, the perpetrator is a family member, and two-thirds of the perpetrators are adult children or spouses.** *(National Center on Elder Abuse. (1998). National elder abuse incidence survey: Executive summary. (Publication #ISBN 0-9100106-63-0). Washington, DC.)*

KNOWING YOUR PARTNER'S HUMAN IMMUNODEFICIENCY VIRUS (HIV) STATUS

Here are some facts about women and HIV taken from Mark Cichocki, RN, on About.com:
- Today, roughly 40 million people worldwide are living with HIV.
- It's estimated that 50 percent of those people living with the disease are **women**.
- While men still make up the majority of HIV cases in the United States, about 300,000 women are living with HIV.
- The proportion of HIV cases that are women has tripled from about 8 to 27 percent since 1985.
- From 2000 to 2004, the number of men living with HIV has increased by 7 percent while the number of women infected has increased 10 percent.

Obviously, HIV affects anyone who has the disease, whether male or female. An HIV diagnosis, while not a death sentence, will most certainly be a life-changing event. However, there are some challenges that are unique to women.

There is an increased risk of reproductive illnesses including vaginal yeast infections, pelvic inflammatory disease (PID), Human Papillomavirus (HPV), and cervical cancer.
- Women often have lower incomes than men or work lower-paying jobs with minimal benefits; women have less access to HIV care and affordable medical insurance.
- Women are more likely to postpone healthcare because of illness or lack of transportation than are men.

- Women assume more family care responsibilities and are more likely to sacrifice their own health care in order to provide for their family, especially their children.

While these statistics are alarming, there is good news. Taking some simple steps can protect you from getting HIV — or prevent women from passing it to others, including their children. While there is no cure, many women with HIV and AIDS are living longer and stronger lives thanks to a number of new treatments. A wide variety of government resources also are in place to help people living with HIV. It is a Champion Woman's responsibility to be tested. Ask pertinent questions before getting in a relationship. Make sure he's tested.

A CREDIT CONVERSATION

There are many credit counseling companies that will help in these tough economic times. Below are some suggestions (taken from Experian.com) that might help improve your credit score.

A credit score reflects credit payment patterns over time, with more emphasis on recent information. Ways to improve a credit score generally include the following:
- Pay your bills on time. Delinquent payments and collections can have a major negative impact on a credit score.
- Keep balances low on credit cards and other "revolving credit." High outstanding debt can affect a credit score.
- Apply for and open new credit accounts only as needed. Don't open accounts just to have a better

credit mix. It probably won't improve your credit score.

Pay off debt rather than moving it around. Also, don't close unused cards as a short-term strategy to improve your credit score. Owing the same amount but having fewer open accounts might lower your credit score.

*"God created you to be a
Champion Woman,
don't settle for anything less."*

Vernon J. Shazier
"The Champion Coach"

REFERENCES

"Anna Quindlen Quotes." *Famous Quotes and Quotations at BrainyQuote*. Web. 26 Apr. 2010. <http://www.brainyquote.com/quotes/authors/a/anna_quindlen_2.html>.

"Build Business Credit at Experian.com." *Credit Report, Credit Score and Credit Check from Experian*. Web. 27 Apr. 2010. <http://www.experian.com/small-business/build-business-credit.jsp>.

"Charles R. Swindoll Quotes." *Find the Famous Quotes You Need, ThinkExist.com Quotations*. Web. 26 Apr. 2010. <http://thinkexist.com/quotation/the_longer_i_live-the_more_i_realize_the_impact/296740.html>.

Cichocki, Mark. "Women and HIV - HIV and Women - HIV - Women." *HIV Symptoms - HIV - The Symptoms of HIV*. Web. 27 Apr. 2010. <http://aids.about.com/od/womensresources/tp/women.htm>.

Covey, Stephen. *The 7 Habits of Highly Effective People*. London: Simon & Schuster, 1999. Print.

"Maya Angelou Quotes." *Famous Quotes and Quotations at BrainyQuote*. Web. 26 Apr. 2010. <http://www.brainyquote.com/quotes/authors/m/maya_angelou.html>.

"Oprah Winfrey Quotes." *Famous Quotes and Quotations at BrainyQuote*. Web. 26 Apr. 2010. <http://www.brainyquote.com/quotes/quotes/o/oprahwinfr133623.html>.

"Peace Pilgrim Quotes." *Find the Famous Quotes You Need, ThinkExist.com Quotations*. Web. 26 Apr. 2010.

<http://thinkexist.com/quotation/when_you_find_pe ace_within_yourself-you_become/294777.html>.

"Phenomenal Woman by Maya Angelou." *PoemHunter.Com - Thousands of Poems and Poets.. Poetry Search Engine*. Web. 27 Apr. 2010. <http://www.poemhunter.com/poem/phenomenal-woman/>.

"Ralph Waldo Emerson Quotes." *Find the Famous Quotes You Need, ThinkExist.com Quotations*. Web. 26 Apr. 2010. <http://thinkexist.com/quotation/to_laugh_often_an d_much-to_win_the_respect_of/255196.html>.

Shah, Mayur. *Free Articles, Information Resources BharatBhasha.com*. Web. 26 Apr. 2010. <http://www.bharatbhasha.com>.

"Thomas A. Edison Quotes." *Famous Quotes and Quotations at BrainyQuote*. Web. 26 Apr. 2010. <http://www.brainyquote.com/quotes/quotes/t/thom asaed149049.html>.

"The Uses of Enchantment: The Meaning and Importance of Fairy Tales by Bruno Bettelheim | LibraryThing." *LibraryThing | Catalog Your Books Online*. Web. 26 Apr. 2010. <http://www.librarything.com/work/432>.

Web. 26 Apr. 2010. <http://www.lyricstime.com/gemma-fox-superstar-lyrics.html>.

"Wilma Rudolph Quotes." *Famous Quotes and Quotations at BrainyQuote*. Web. 26 Apr. 2010. <http://www.brainyquote.com/quotes/authors/w/wil ma_rudolph.html>.

About the Author
"The Champion Coach"

Vernon J. Shazier is the Executive Pastor at Mount Bethel Ministries located in Ft. Lauderdale/Ft. Pierce, Florida. He is an innovative leader and performance coach who upholds the highest standards of personal and professional integrity. He is committed to helping individuals and leaders of small and large organizations reach "**Championship Status**". He is sought after throughout the country as a motivational speaker and lecturer in the areas of leadership and staff development. He possesses outstanding speaking skills and has an unwavering dedication to *Excellence*.

He holds a degree in Bio-Medical Engineering from Kieser University, a Bachelor of Science in Psychology from Nova Southeastern University. He is also a graduate of George W. Truett Theological Seminary, Baylor University in Waco, Texas, where he received a Master of Divinity in Theology.

WWW.THECHAMPIONWOMAN.COM

THE CHAMPION WOMAN SEMINARS

These experiential and exciting seminars are designed to empower women as mothers, wives, professionals and entrepreneurs from all walks of life. After attending The Champion Woman Seminar, you will be equipped and empowered with strategies that will propel you to "Championship Status" as a woman.

Please fill out the Booking form and submit your request at www.thechampionwoman.com. It is greatly appreciated and should you have any questions or require more information, please feel free to contact us at **info@thechampionleader.com**.

THE CHAMPION WOMAN PARTNERS

What is a Partner?

A partner is "one who shares responsibilities in common activity with another individual or group."

How does your partnership benefit The Champion Woman?

The Champion Woman is designed to empower women as mothers, wives, professionals and entrepreneurs from all walks of life. As a partner with The Champion Woman you can help us reach millions of other woman. Your donations will be used to support our efforts throughout various media outlets including Television, Radio, Newsletters and the Internet. Your gifts will also allow The Champion Woman team to travel all over the world to help equip and empower with strategies that will propel woman to "Championship Status."

How does partnering with The Champion Woman benefit you?

Your partnership ensures that you will receive:

> Spiritual covering through covenant prayer for you and your family or organization.

> Periodic gift items and ministry tools given to thank our partners for their continued pledges.

Satisfaction of knowing that lives are being transformed because of you.

Thank you for your interest in becoming a Champion Woman Partner. We take our partnership with you seriously and will work diligently to sustain our covenant with you and with those whose lives will be changed by this ministry.

BECOME A PARTNER TODAY!
WWW.THECHAMPIONWOMAN.COM

Champion Leader Products

How to Build A Championship Team
Paperback Book and Audiobook

The Champion Leader Motivator Series
101 Champion Leadership Quotes

Available at: www.thechampionleader.com

www.ingramcontent.com/pod-product-compliance
Lightning Source LLC
Chambersburg PA
CBHW051451290426
44109CB00016B/1710